CHRIST
THE KING
LORD OF HISTORY
WORKBOOK
and Study Guide

—With Answer Key—

D1567924

CHRIST THE KING

LORD OF HISTORY

WORKBOOK

and Study Guide

—With Answer Key—

By

Belinda Mooney

Based on the text by
Anne W. Carroll

TAN BOOKS AND PUBLISHERS, INC.
Rockford, Illinois 61105

Copyright © 2000 by Belinda Mooney.

ISBN 0-89555-673-1

Library of Congress Control No.: 00-131585

Cover illustration: The Coronation of Charlemagne, by von Kaulbach. Collection of the Stiftung Maximilianeum, Munich.

All rights reserved. No part of this book may be reproduced or transmitted in any form or by any means, electronic or mechanical, including photocopying, recording, or by any information storage or retrieval system, without permission in writing from the Publisher.

Printed and bound in the United States of America.

TAN BOOKS AND PUBLISHERS, INC.
P.O. Box 424
Rockford, Illinois 61105
2000

Dedication

In Honor of the Most Holy Name
and in Adoration of the
Most Holy Face of Jesus Christ.

We Praise You, Lord,
We Bless Your Holy Name,
We Adore Your Holy Face.
We deeply desire to walk in the light of Your Face
all the days of our lives.

Acknowledgments

I am deeply grateful to my family for their patience and help in preparing the manuscript as well as for allowing me the time I needed to do the work, which was often very detailed and sometimes tedious. I thank my extended family for all the confidence they have in me. I thank all of my home schooling friends for their witness and example in raising their children in the Catholic Faith. I thank Mary Frances Lester of TAN for her encouragement and help.

I thank Our Blessed Mother Mary for her intercession. I thank St. Raphael for his intercession. I thank my dear sweet Lord Jesus for His gifts and His permission to write again. I thank the Holy Spirit for all of the inspiration needed to write the book and for the fortitude to finish. I thank God my Father for allowing me to know Him from so early an age and for always being with me.

Contents

A Message to the Student

Welcome to this *Workbook* for *Christ the King—Lord of History*. This workbook was designed to help you make good use of Anne Carroll's textbook, *Christ the King—Lord of History*, which is an excellent text for understanding the basics of world history from a Catholic perspective.

Mrs. Carroll recommends using her text for a two-year course of world history, and I concur. Whether you are a student or an adult, it is more important to learn this material thoroughly than to go through it quickly. This thorough grasp of world history is fundamental to understanding our Catholic Faith; it is also fundamental to understanding the history of America, the New World.

Christ the King—Lord of History is not a text to simply read through and then expect yourself to remember. Without some sort of reinforcement, the material will simply become a blur in your mind. In order to remember the information and to see how the history of the world is intimately linked with that of the Catholic Church, you have to continue to work through the material and have it presented in different formats. I have created this *Workbook* for *Christ the King—Lord of History* to help you go over the material. This *Workbook* covers almost every major topic from the text.

Whether you are an adult working independently to learn history or a student in a Catholic school or home school, I recommend that you use the Workbook as a guide before you go through each chapter, to assist you in focusing on the most important material, and then answer the questions once you have finished. Later, you could use the *Workbook* with the answers filled in as a review. In that scenario, you are really studying the material in-depth three times besides reading the chapter!

An alternate way to use this *Workbook* would be to use the Questions as a test at the end of each chapter. The three sheets of paper (five or six sides) for each chapter can be cut out of the book if desired. The Answer Key pages are perforated for easy removal.

Study Tips

When you read *Christ the King—Lord of History*, take the initiative in learning and remembering the material! Take notes as you read through the text. Brief notes in the form of words, phrases and dates can be so useful and will not stop your progress in reading the chapter (the way copying a whole sentence would). For more complicated material, it is highly recommended that you make yourself time-lines and charts to organize it for clearer understanding and better retention. For example, if you make a table or chart with names and dates of the successors to Queen Elizabeth I, you can see them at a glance and remember them more easily.

Christ the King—Lord of History is not completely chronological by chapter, but is organized by periods of time, periods in Church History, and by countries. The author sometimes covers several hundred years in one chapter and then, in the next chapter, goes back 100 years or so to relate what was happening in another country at that same time. When you come to a part in the text that fits in with something read in an earlier chapter, go back and look it up before going on, so that you really understand. Make sure that you go back to the preceding chapter and see how the current chapter fits with the preceding one, how it completes and continues the information studied previously. If you feel confused, take the tables and charts you have made from each chapter and set them side by side by time period to see the information more clearly. Review the two chapters together when you finish reading to make sure you understand how they fit and where they overlap. For example, put together the different sections on the Holy Shroud found in various chapters (by marking the pages and flipping back and forth through the four or five chapters), so you get a complete picture. See pages xii–xiv for some sample charts. You can make simple charts like this for yourself whenever the data presented in the text is difficult to remember.

Sometimes a person who was mentioned in an earlier chapter will pop up again in a later one with the surname only. It will seem as though you have seen this name somewhere, but you cannot remember where. Don't keep reading; stop and go back to find who this is and in what context you read about him or her earlier.

Continued Learning

It can be so much fun to branch out with continued learning. At the end of many chapters are listed lives of saints from that particular time period, and possibly other books that fit the time period. Those by Mary Fabyan Windeatt are written for younger readers (age 10 and up). Those by F.A. Forbes were originally written for young people in their teens, but they are not "juvenile," and adults enjoy them as well. You can also look up events, people, terms, etc. in a Catholic dictionary or Catholic encyclopedia, even if you feel that you understand them. These sources will probably have additional information.

As you work through the chapters in the text, consider reading extra material (even beyond what I have suggested) to solidify your learning and continue to jog your memory. I would recommend Bible passages, readings from the Church Fathers and Popes in the Divine Office or Liturgy of the Hours, and books that provide more in-depth coverage of a particular part in the text. For example, after Chapter 17 on the Protestant Revolt, you might read from the Bible about obedience in *Ecclesiasticus* (*Sirach*) and in the Passion narratives of *Matthew, Mark, Luke* and *John* (Our Lord's obedience).

An excellent resource for continued learning is Dr. Warren Carroll's multi-volume *The History of Christendom*, available from Christendom Press (134 Christendom Dr. Front Royal, Virginia 22630). You can obtain other materials from good Catholic publishers like TAN; for out-of-print books, you can use Inter-library Loan through your public library. This will allow you to receive books from libraries around the country after a short waiting time (approximately three weeks). Church libraries, university libraries and family and friends may also allow you to borrow and read books related to the chapter. For example, you could read Hilaire Belloc's *How the Reformation*

Happened. Reading material from Catholic publishers will help you to recognize more easily when other books are written from a Protestant or atheist perspective. You will see how those works have indoctrinated our society as opposed to the truth.

Study Chapters 17, 18 and 20 in great depth and very carefully. Do not move on in the text until you really understand these chapters, as they are critical to understanding the Protestant Revolt and the corresponding devastation to God's Kingdom that we see today. For this reason, I have suggested a greater number of books for Chapter 20. Take your time. Your understanding and knowledge will assist you during your life in your evangelization efforts, as well as in withstanding errors and responding to non-Catholic evangelizers.

The Catholic Meaning of History

Remember, the more times you see the information in different forms, the better you will retain it and the more clearly you will understand history. Eventually you will feel as though you are on a road with a clear sense of your direction, knowing and understanding what is to the north, south, east and west. You will see clearly what happened before you in history and what is happening now. You will understand how we got to where we are today. You will see how God has worked through so many individual people and how people have affected history because of their cooperation or lack of cooperation to His Will.

When you see what individuals like Luther and Cardinal Richelieu have brought about by their disobedience and the devastating effects they have had on all of us down to the present, it will become clear that the price of disobedience is death for many souls. On the other hand, obedience—as Jesus and all of His saints show us—brings blessings, graces and goodness to others, and many souls are saved. Through this clear Catholic understanding of history, you will better understand how important it is that you cooperate with God's grace and do His will—not only for your own soul, but also for the sake of others, including those living now and those in times to come.

I hope that my efforts to make Mrs. Carroll's text more useful to you will help you to truly be all that God wants you to be for the Church. May God make clear to you, through the gifts of the Holy Spirit (knowledge, wisdom and understanding), the history of His world and Church that you are about to study. I will be praying for you and I ask your prayers for me. God bless you.

—Mrs. Belinda Mooney

Timeline of Major Events in World History

	GOD'S COVENANT WITH ABRAHAM
	SINAI COVENANT—God gives the 10 Commandments to Moses
510 B.C.	FOUNDING OF THE ROMAN EMPIRE
457–429 B.C.	GOLDEN AGE OF GREECE
1 A.D.	THE INCARNATION: Jesus comes into the world
33 A.D.	FOUNDING OF CATHOLIC CHURCH
450–1050	THE "DARK AGES" (approximate dates)
800	CORONATION OF CHARLEMAGNE by Pope Leo III (Beginning of Holy Roman Empire)
1050–1450	THE "HIGH MIDDLE AGES" (approximate dates)
1054	GREEK SCHISM—Patriarch of Constantinople refused to accept papal authority. Russian and Greek Orthodox Churches separate from the Roman Catholic Church.
1453	FALL OF CONSTANTINOPLE, and thus the fall of the Roman Empire in the East
1492	EXPULSION OF THE MOORS (MOSLEMS) FROM SPAIN
1492	COLUMBUS' VOYAGE TO THE NEW WORLD
1517	PROTESTANT REVOLT—Martin Luther nails his "95 Theses" to the door of the Church in Wittenberg, beginning a series of events that would launch the Protestant Revolt.
1534	ACT OF SUPREMACY, ENGLAND—Henry VIII formally took England into schism by declaring himself head of the Church in England.
1571	LEPANTO—Christian victory over the Turks at Lepanto, protecting Europe from Moslem rule.
1600	SCIENTIFIC REVOLUTION—discoveries by Isaac Newton and others. (approximate date)
1648	TREATY OF WESTPHALIA—This ended the Thirty Years War and marked a permanent split in Christendom between Protestant areas and Catholic areas.
1700's	LIBERALISM, ABSOLUTISM AND FREEMASONRY attack the Church. 18th century—"Age of Reason" or "Enlightenment."

CHRIST THE KING, LORD OF HISTORY — WORKBOOK

1769 INDUSTRIAL REVOLUTION begins with the invention of the steam engine.

1789 THE FRENCH REVOLUTION, dated from "the storming of the Bastille"

1820's SOCIALISM appears in France and England, demanding that government control the means of production and own and operate factories and businesses.

1848 COMMUNISM—publication of *The Communist Manifesto*, written by Karl Marx and Friedrich Engels.

1914–1918 WORLD WAR I

1917 OUR LADY OF FATIMA appears; RUSSIAN REVOLUTION begins— Our Lady appeals for prayer and sacrifices to prevent spread of "the errors of Russia" throughout the world, plus wars and persecutions of the Church. The Russian Revolution ushers in Communism in Russia.

1936–1939 SPANISH CIVIL WAR—Franco and the Nationalist forces overcome the Communist forces in Spain.

1939–1945 WORLD WAR II

1965–1973 WAR IN VIETNAM

1962–1965 VATICAN COUNCIL II—Afterwards, Modernist ideas were held up as being in "the spirit of Vatican II"; concept became common that anything "pre-Vatican II" was outdated.

1978 JOHN PAUL II BECOMES POPE

A History of the Holy Shroud
(Pages 77–78; 83–84; 156–157; 199–200)

Pre-57 A.D. St. Jude brings the Shroud to Edessa to cure King Abgar and establish Christianity there (baptized the King and others).

57 A.D. persecutions of Christians broke out; cloth hidden in city gates for safe-keeping

57 A.D.–6th century In Edessa

6th century Edessa had an earthquake which damaged the city walls and revealed the hiding place of the Shroud. It is enshrined in main church.

943 General John Curcuas brought it to Constantinople for Byzantine Emperor Romanus Lecapenus. It was installed in the royal chapel and not shown publicly until it was unfolded and found to be a Shroud, not just a portrait. Later, it was used in a ceremony representing Christ's Resurrection on Easter Sunday.

1356 Jeanne DeCharney exhibited Shroud—first time seen publicly in 150 years.

1532 Fire in the Church in Chambery, France

1578 House of Savoy moved to Turin, Italy and exhibited Shroud there.

1983 Last Savoy relative dies and wills the Shroud to the Vatican

Succession of The English Throne—Stuart Reign

Elizabeth—Protestant

James I (Stuart)—Protestant

Charles I (Stuart)—Protestant—married a Catholic

Oliver Cromwell—Protestant

Charles II (Stuart)—Protestant—married a Catholic

James II (Stuart)—Catholic

Mary (Stuart) and William III of Orange—Protestant

Anne (Stuart)—Protestant

George of Hanover—Protestant

CHRIST
THE KING
LORD OF HISTORY
WORKBOOK
and Study Guide

—With Answer Key—

Perfect Score: 100
(Each Question is worth 2 points.)

Score: _____

Completion

Directions: Complete and make each statement true and accurate by writing one or more words on each blank line.

1. History is the _____ of _____ , which have made a difference in the world.

2. Men who write history are called _____.

3. Each _____ will write about the events he thinks are most important and will give his own _____ .

4. Jesus was not only a religious figure; he was a _____ figure as well.

5. The only event which has influenced every single person who has ever lived is the _____ of Jesus Christ.

6. Geography is very important because we cannot fully understand events unless we know _____ these events occurred.

7. Europe and the Middle East have produced the greatest _____ and have had the most _____ on the rest of the world.

8. B.C. stands for _____ .

9. *Anno Domini* is Latin for _____ .

10. The _____ dates with higher numbers occurred before those with lower numbers.

11. Around the year _____ B.C., God began to act directly in history in preparation for the Incarnation.

12. The years before 3000 B.C. are known as _____ times.

13. One of the main reference books you will need is _____ .

14. The Old Testament in Protestant Bibles includes only those books originally written in the _____ language.

Multiple Choice

Directions: After each statement below, there is a set of words or phrases. Circle the letter next to the one word or phrase that best completes the sentence.

1. History includes
   a) the bombing of Pearl Harbor
   b) a couple celebrating 10 yrs. of marriage
   c) Columbus discovering America
   d) a. and c.
   e) all of the above

2. The most important event in the history of the world had influence
   a) at the time it occurred
   b) at the present time
   c) even before it occurred
   d) all of the above

3. The people who prepared the world for the coming of Jesus were
   a) Egyptian
   b) Babylonian
   c) Jewish
   d) Roman

4. *Christ the King—Lord of History* covers:
   a) what events happened and why
   b) what resulted from the events
   c) what difference the events made
   d) great people who have made history
   e) a, b, and c
   f) all of the above

5. The globe is divided for convenience into
   a) continents
   b) hemispheres
   c) oceans
   d) land masses

6. The great land masses of the world are the seven
   a) empires
   b) kingdoms
   c) continents
   d) nations

7. The United States was too small to make much of a difference in world events until about
      a) 1776
      b) 1865
      c) 1917
      d) 1945

8. The last year dated B.C. was 1 B.C. It was followed by what year A.D.?
      a) 0
      b) 1
      c) 2
      d) none of the above

9. The Bible was originally written in
      a) Hebrew and Greek
      b) Hebrew and Latin
      c) Hebrew only
      d) Greek and Latin

10. This history book spends less time on which country?
      a) Spain
      b) United States
      c) France
      d) Egypt

True/False

Directions: Circle the letter T if the statement is true or F if the statement is false.

1.   T   F   All events make up history.

2.   T   F   All historians have similar ideas about what events should be recorded.

3.   T   F   It is possible to create a perfect history of the Civil War.

4.   T   F   The Church is the only institution which survived the collapse of Roman Civilization.

5.   T   F   Many of the problems which our world presently faces are caused by the rejection of the Church and its teachings.

6.   T   F   The best history books are those which emphasize wars because history only makes sense from that point of view.

7.   T   F   Because geography can be confusing, it is not very important.

8.   T   F   The first two digits of a year indicate the century that it is in (e.g., 1705 is in the 17th century).

9.   T   F   The argument that the Bible is a collection of stories that did not really happen has been proved wrong by archeological excavations.

10.   T   F   There are different versions of the Bible based on different translations of the original languages.

11.   T   F   The Bible used by the Catholic Church includes the books originally written in both Hebrew and Greek.

12.   T   F   Protestant Bibles have fewer books in the Old Testament than Catholic Bibles.

13.   T   F   The Bible may be used as a history book.

Matching

Directions: This list is made up of names of persons, groups, places and things. Each one corresponds to one of the lettered phrases below. In each blank, write the letter of the phrase that correctly identifies that person, group, place or thing.

1. ___ C.E.

2. ___ The Incarnation

3. ___ Empire

4. ___ Babylon

5. ___ Alexander the Great

6. ___ Tacitus

7. ___ Western civilization

8. ___ B.C.

9. ___ A.D.

10. ___ Josephus

11. ___ Napoleon

12. ___ 1 A.D. to 100 A.D.

13. ___ King James version

A) Before Christ
B) conquered an empire against great odds
C) non-Christian abbreviation for the time we are living in now

D) most important event in history
E) Jewish historian
F) a nation which rules other nations
G) first century
H) Year of Our Lord

I) Protestant Bible
J) dominated Europe for many years
K) great empire
L) Catholic civilization
M) Roman historian

Mini-Essay Question:
(Extra credit—4 points.)

Why does the Catholic Bible contain seven more books than the Protestant Bible?

Personal Opinion:

Name an important or interesting fact that you learned in this chapter. How could this fact affect your life?

Supplemental Reading

Fr. John Laux. *Introduction to the Bible.* TAN.

Rev. Henry Graham. *Where We Got the Bible—Our Debt to the Catholic Church.* TAN.

Douay-Rheims version. *The Holy Bible.* TAN.

CHRIST THE KING, LORD OF HISTORY — WORKBOOK

Perfect Score: 100
(Each Question is worth 2 points.)

Score: _____

Completion

Directions: Complete and make each statement true and accurate by writing one or more words on each blank line.

1. The new food supplies made available by the _____ made possible a great increase in _____ and laid the foundations for civilization.

2. Civilization is distinguished from barbarism by the presence of true _____ and the use of _____ .

3. Each of the great cities of the Sumerian civilization (Agade, Ur, Babylon) was once a mighty center of _____ and _____ .

4. The Egyptians learned to write from the _____ .

5. India was the only civilized culture known to have institutionalized enforced cremation, through a practice known as _____ .

6. Because of the Indians' philosophy and their belief in _____ , they could not believe in the value of the individual human person.

7. God made with Abraham a _____ , a solemn agreement which binds the persons involved to each other.

8. In ancient times Canaan was the center of the human world—the point nearest to the great concentrations of population, a crossroads and a juncture among _____ , Asia and _____ .

9. In order for him to receive the great reward which God had prepared for him, Abraham had to prove his _____ and _____ in the Lord beyond any shadow of a doubt.

10. God said to Abraham through the angel: "And in thy seed shall all the nations of the earth be blessed, because thou has _____ my voice."

11. Abraham's faith in God was _____ . He believed that somehow both he and his son _____ would return. And so they did.

12. Abraham is the spiritual father of one and one half _____ living human beings.

13. Abraham was buried in a tomb in Hebron, the location of which is marked today by a _____ .

14. _____ was sold by his brothers to wandering slave traders who brought him into Egypt.

Multiple Choice

Directions: After each statement below, there is a set of words or phrases. Circle the letter next to the one word or phrase that best completes the sentence.

1. The first civilizations grew up in
   a) cities
   b) river valleys
   c) deserts
   d) none of the above

2. There were three river valley civilizations in ancient times:
   a) Mesopotamia (Iraq), Egypt and Harappa (India)
   b) Mesopotamia, Egypt and Greece
   c) Mesopotamia, Harappa and Israel
   d) Egypt, Harappa and Greece

3. The earliest civilization began in the fertile lands between the Tigris and Euphrates Rivers and is called what civilization?
   a) Indian
   b) Egyptian
   c) Harappan
   d) Sumerian

4. Egypt was from the beginning ruled as a
   a) democracy
   b) republic
   c) dictatorship
   d) none of the above

5. When India was first opened to the West, the many evils found there, which apparently originated in Harappa, included
    a) the cult of Kali
    b) self-torture
    c) belief in the pharaoh as a god
    d) a. and b. only
    e) a. and c. only

6. To whom did God choose to begin the revelation of the divine plan for the Redemption of men?
    a) Moses
    b) Abraham
    c) John the Baptist
    d) Isaias

7. The land to which God sent Abraham was Canaan. Which of the following is not another name for Canaan?
    a) Palestine
    b) Holy Land
    c) Israel
    d) Promised Land
    e) Mesopotamia

8. This book in the Bible tells us the story of Abraham's trust in God, which led him to say yes to the sacrifice of his son Isaac:
    a) Genesis
    b) Exodus
    c) Leviticus
    d) none of the above

9. After the angel appeared in order to tell Abraham to spare Isaac, Abraham lifted his eyes and saw behind his back this animal, which he took and offered as a holocaust instead of his son:
    a) a goat
    b) a lion
    c) a ram
    d) a lamb
    e) none of the above

10. The members of what religion(s) call Abraham their spiritual father?
    a) Christian
    b) Moslem
    c) Jewish
    d) a. and c.
    e) all of the above

True/False

Directions: Circle the letter T if the statement is true or F if the statement is false.

1.   T   F   River valleys had better soil and easy availability of water, which made farming easier.

2.   T   F   The earliest civilization began around 2000 B.C.

3.   T   F   The remains of a temple, called a ziggurat (shaped like a stepped pyramid), is virtually all that remains of the first civilization in the world.

4.   T   F   The civilization of Babylon grew up along the Nile River in Africa.

5.   T   F   Because Egypt is a narrow strip of land surrounded by desert, it is not very fertile.

6.   T   F   Harappan traders reached Sumeria, where canal irrigation, deep plowing and well-made metal tools were in use, and Harappa adopted these improvements.

7.   T   F   There have been few men who have towered above history as Abraham has, who have made decisions and taken actions which influenced millions of people thousands of years after their death.

8.   T   F   God promised Abraham he would have only one descendent, named Isaac.

9.   T   F   God appeared to Abraham as one Man so that he could understand that God is One rather than many.

10.   T   F   Abraham hesitated briefly to do God's will.

11.   T   F   Abraham is honored by four religions which call him their father.

12.   T   F   Because of his talents and ability to interpret dreams, Joseph rose to a high place in the Hyksos government.

13.   T   F   After Joseph's prudent advice spared Egypt the effects of the famine, the 12 tribes took up residence in Egypt.

Matching

Directions: This list is made up of names of persons, groups, places and things. Each one corresponds to one of the lettered phrases below. In each blank, write the letter of the phrase that correctly identifies that person, group, place or thing.

1. ___ Mesopotamia and Palestine

2. ___ Sargon of Agade

3. ___ Temple near Ur

4. ___ Harappa civilization

5. ___ Caste system

6. ___ Abram

7. ___ Canaan

8. ___ Sarah

9. ___ Hebron

10. ___ Mount Moriah

11. ___ mosque

12. ___ Nation of Israel

13. ___ Akhenaten

A) fierce warrior
B) India
C) place of Abraham's sacrifice of Isaac
D) Iraq and Israel
E) wife of Abraham

F) 14th–century B.C. King of Egypt
G) ruins of Sumerian civilization
H) Jewish people
I) rigid social classes

J) an oasis, where God appeared to Abraham
K) Promised Land
L) Abraham
M) Moslem place of worship

Mini-Essay Question:
(Extra credit—4 points.)

What did Abraham reveal about himself through his willingness to sacrifice his son to God?

Personal Opinion:

Name an important or interesting fact that you learned in this chapter. How could this fact affect your life?

Perfect Score: 100
(Each Question is worth 2 points.)

Score: _____

Completion

Directions: Complete and make each statement true and accurate by writing one or more words on each blank line.

1. The Pharaohs _____ and _____ built new cities on which the Israelite slaves labored.

2. God is _____ being, which means He owes His existence to no one or nothing else.

3. The method chosen by God to persuade both the people and the pharaoh to heed Moses was to bring about a series of catastrophes, the ten

   _____ .

4. By using _____ phenomena to bring about the liberation of His people, God demonstrated to the Israelites and Egyptians alike that He was

   the Lord of _____ .

5. God commanded the people to be ready to march, so they ate their final meal

   dressed for a _____ .

6. The Passover feast would foreshadow Jesus' freeing of all men from the slavery

   of _____ through His Blood.

7. The Israelites were guided in their journey by a pillar of _____

   by day and a pillar of _____ by night.

8. The Jewish people would _____ each time there was a crisis, yet God continued to provide them overwhelming evidence of His loving

   _____ .

9. Moses lead the people across the desert from one _____ and well to another.

10. God promised Israel He would count them a Kingdom of _____ , a consecrated nation.

11. _____ were a huge departure from established behavior.

12. The people ratified the covenent with a _____ .

13. Moses turned away God's anger by _____ , and Israel again promised loyalty to God.

14. _____ and _____ were the only two Israelites whose faith and courage had never failed in the desert.

Multiple Choice

Directions: After each statement below, there is a set of words or phrases. Circle the letter next to the one word or phrase that best completes the sentence.

1. Moses was brought up in the Egyptian court, as we know from the Book of
   - a) Genesis
   - b) Exodus
   - c) Leviticus
   - d) Numbers

2. The name Yahweh means
   - a) God of Jacob
   - b) Promised One
   - c) God with us
   - d) I Am

3. The number of plagues God sent upon Egypt was
   - a) three
   - b) five
   - c) ten
   - d) fifteen

4. The plague of locusts mocked the goddess
   - a) Serapis
   - b) Beelzebul
   - c) Heeate
   - d) Aten

5. God commanded that the Israelites
        a) kill a lamb and eat all of it
        b) bake leavened bread
        c) put the blood of the lamb on their doorposts
        d) a. and c. only
        e) all of the above

6. To celebrate the night that the angel of death spared the Israelites and killed only the first-born *Egyptians*, Jewish people yearly celebrate
        a) Yom Kippur
        b) Hanukkah
        c) Passover
        d) none of the above

7. God's miracles in the desert included all the following except
        a) changing bitter water to sweet
        b) providing lambs and quail for food
        c) producing water from a rock
        d) helping them defeat an enemy tribe

8. God delivered the Ten Commandments with
        a) a thunderstorm
        b) lightning bolts
        c) a fire on the mountain
        d) b. and c. only
        e) none of the above

9. To punish the Israelites' lack of faith and trust, God decreed that no one older than this (except for two men) would enter the Promised Land:
        a) 10 years old
        b) 20 years old
        c) 30 years old
        d) 40 years old

10. He is the chief human author of the Pentateuch, the first 5 books of the Bible:
        a) Moses
        b) Abraham
        c) Joshua
        d) Caleb

True/False

Directions: Circle the letter T if the statement is true or F if the statement is false.

1.   T   F   Rameses II reigned for 70 years.

2. T   F   During his reign, Rameses II was the most powerful man in the world.

3. T   F   God is existence itself; His name is I Am.

4. T   F   The blood-red Nile was an attack on the worship of the god Re.

5. T   F   The Israelites chose the route through Sinai instead of along the Mediterranean.

6. T   F   The pillars of cloud and fire are signs in the Scriptures of the presence of God.

7. T   F   The Israelites learned of Pharaoh's pursuit of them as they camped near the Red Sea.

8. T   F   The Israelites' part of the Sinai Covenant was to keep the Ten Commandments.

9. T   F   The Israelites stayed for 40 years at the camp while Moses received the Ten Commandments.

10. T   F   After the Israelites were given the Ten Commandments, Moses returned to the mountain.

11. T   F   For 50 years, the Israelites 20 years and older wandered in the Sinai desert as punishment for their lack of faith.

12. T   F   Moses trained the new generation for battle before they entered the Promised Land.

13. T   F   After Moses died, Joshua assumed leadership of Israel.

Matching

Directions: This list is made up of names of persons, groups, places and things. Each one corresponds to one of the lettered phrases below. In each blank, write the letter of the phrase that correctly identifies that person, group, place or thing.

1. ___ General Horemheb

2. ___ dynasty

3. ___ Moses

4. ___ Sinai peninsula

5. ___ Yahweh

6. ___ plagues

7. ___ Passover time

8. ___ Angel of death

9. ___ Sinai

10. ___ Sinai Covenant

11. ___ The Ten Commandments

12. ___ idolatry

13. ___ Ark of the Covenant

A) a code of law
B) late March or early April
C) desert
D) new agreement between God and Israel
E) liberator
F) killed all firstborn Egyptians
G) located between Egypt and Palestine
H) ruling family
I) name God gave Himself
J) restored the god-king's empire
K) catastrophes
L) beautiful box containing the Commandment tablets
M) worship of false gods

Mini-Essay Question: What is the connection between the first Passover and Jesus Christ dying on the Cross?
(Extra credit—4 points.)

Personal Opinion: Name an important or interesting fact that you learned in this chapter. How could this fact affect your life?

Supplemental Reading

Johnson, Hannan, Dominica. *Bible History*. TAN.

Bible. *Exodus* 20:1–17.
   Leviticus 19:1–18, 31–37. (Ten Commandments)

Perfect Score: 100
(Each Question is worth 2 points.)

Score: _____

Completion

Directions: Complete and make each statement true and accurate by writing one or more words on each blank line.

1. _____ led his people across the Jordan River into Canaan where the 12 tribes of Israel settled in the Promised Land.

2. Joshua warned the people to choose no earthly _____ .

3. _____ drove the Philistines from the Promised Land.

4. David conquered _____ , where he established his capital city and brought the Ark of the Covenant.

5. God honored David by granting him a vision of a future _____ , one who would be descended from David himself and who would establish an everlasting kingdom.

6. As long as David was _____ to God, he was the greatest king in the world. He saw his world crumble when he used his power to

   _____ .

7. History teaches that earthly power and success cannot bring lasting

   _____ .

8. When the nation of Israel split, the northern kingdom was called

   _____ and the southern kingdom was called

   _____ .

9. _____ was the setting of the challenge of Elias to the 450 priests of Baal.

10. _____ was taken up to Heaven in a fiery chariot after having faithfully completed his work.

11. God sent holy men called _____ to Judah to point out the people's sins and to foretell disasters that would result from their sins.

12. _____ responded to God's call with the words, "Here I am, send me."

13. The first main prophet of the exiled Israelites in Babylon was _____ .

14. Upon their return from exile, the Jews again realized they were the _____ and had a special purpose in history.

Multiple Choice

Directions: After each statement below, there is a set of words or phrases. Circle the letter next to the one word or phrase that best completes the sentence.

1. Leaders who assumed responsibility for Israel during emergencies were called
    a) kings
    b) judges
    c) warriors
    d) anointed ones
    e) none of the above

2. The Israelites were defeated by the Philistines and ruled by them for a period of
    a) 40 years
    b) 100 years
    c) 300 years
    d) 500 years
    e) none of the above

3. David was anointed King of Israel at the age of
    a) 30
    b) 35
    c) 40
    d) 50
    e) none of the above

4. The king who committed sins involving Bathsheba and Uriah was
    a) Saul
    b) David
    c) Solomon
    d) Rehoboam
    e) none of the above

5. Solomon's Temple in Jerusalem was dedicated about the year
     a) 950 B.C.
     b) 700 B.C.
     c) 500 B.C.
     d) 100 B.C.
     e) none of the above

6. The northern kingdom of Israel was destroyed by
     a) famine
     b) earthquakes
     c) conquest by the Assyrians
     d) civil war
     e) c. and d.

7. Like Abraham and Moses, this prophet received a personal visitation from God:
     a) Elias
     b) Isaias
     c) Ezechiel
     d) Daniel
     e) none of the above

8. The prophet who foretold the destruction of Judah, the deportation of its citizens, their return, and the future sufferings and resurrection of Christ was
     a) Elias
     b) Isaias
     c) Ezechiel
     d) Daniel
     e) none of the above

9. The king of Judah gave Assyria control over Judah's affairs in exchange for protection from Assyria. This is called
     a) protectionism
     b) colonization
     c) vassalage
     d) none of the above

10. The prediction that Cyrus, King of the Persians, would defeat the Babylonians was revealed through mysterious handwriting on the wall, which was interpreted by
     a) Ezechiel
     b) Daniel
     c) Zoroaster
     d) Isaias

True/False

Directions: Circle the letter T if the statement is true or F if the statement is false.

1. T   F   Before he died, Joshua approved of the people choosing an earthly king.

2. T   F   Saul had the authority to rule the people and the responsibility to rule in harmony with God's Will.

3. T   F   Saul was humble and accepted God's Will.

4. T   F   Saul was the greatest of all the Kings of Israel.

5. T   F   God taught us through David that He can still use weak and sinful people to accomplish His Will.

6. T   F   Solomon's 40 years as a ruler were marked by strife with other lands.

7. T   F   Solomon eventually became too attached to his wealth and prestige.

8. T   F   Jezebel tried to enforce the worship of pagan gods throughout Israel.

9. T   F   An angel touched Isaias' lips with a burning coal, and Isaias welcomed the pain as a sign to mark that his sins were forgiven.

10. T   F   God pressed Isaias into service, despite unwillingness on Isaias' part.

11. T   F   The Babylonians captured Jerusalem but had mercy on the people.

12. T   F   The prophets helped the people to see their misfortunes and disasters in terms of just punishment for their sins and to realize that they must turn back to God and worship Him.

13. T   F   The Persian King Cyrus allowed the Chosen People to return home.

Matching

Directions: This list is made up of names of persons, groups, places and things. Each one corresponds to one of the lettered phrases below. In each blank, write the letter of the phrase that correctly identifies that person, group, place or thing.

1. ___ Canaanites

2. ___ Palestine

3. ___ Samuel

4. ___ Saul

5. ___ David

6. ___ Messiah

7. ___ Psalms

8. ___ Absalom

9. ___ Temple of Yahweh

10. ___ Rehoboam

11. ___ Jezebel

12. ___ The Exile

13. ___ Daniel

A) served as Judge under
   Philistine oppression
B) second King of Israel
C) stronger personality
   than Achab
D) named for warriors
   who defeated Israel

E) Babylonian Captivity
F) poems of David
G) ordered built by Solomon
H) had ability to
   interpret dreams
I) Anointed One
J) Folly of the Nation

K) enemies of Israel
L) first King of Israel
M) David's son

Mini-Essay Question:
(Extra credit—4 points.)

King Cyrus was kind to the Jews, unlike other ancient conquerors. What is a possible reason for his high moral code?

Personal Opinion:

Name an important or interesting fact that you learned in this chapter. How could this fact affect your life?

Supplemental Reading

Johnson, Hannan, Dominica. *Bible History*. TAN.

Mary Fabyan Windeatt. *King David and His Songs*. TAN.

CHRIST THE KING, LORD OF HISTORY — WORKBOOK

Perfect Score: 100
(Each Question is worth 2 points.)

Score: _____

Completion

Directions: Complete and make each statement true and accurate by writing one or more words on each blank line.

1. Greece was divided into _____ , which were a series of independent cities which ruled the territory surrounding them.

2. The battle in which 6,400 Persians died in trying to capture Greece was fought on the plain of _____ .

3. Athens appealed to _____ for help against Xerxes.

4. The time of great artistic and cultural achievements in Greece is known as its _____ .

5. The Greek scientist _____ made advances in geometry, while _____ made advances in medicine.

6. The development of _____ , the use of reason and logic to study the great questions of the universe, was among the greatest Greek achievements.

7. The Greek philosophers taught us how to think logically about questions and problems, using our minds to find _____ and _____ .

8. Western civilization, based in _____ , was able to advance in science and medicine because of the use of reason and logic.

9. The doctrines of the Church can be defended _____ and can be better understood through the use of _____ .

10. After Philip the Great was assassinated, his son _____ became the king of Macedon and Greece at the age of 20.

11. Alexander had been tutored by _____ .

12. Alexander wanted to march to the _____ of the _____ .

13. Alexander married _____ , daughter of the Sogdian commander.

14. After Alexander died, Macedon, _____ and _____ were the three great powers in the world.

Multiple Choice

Directions: After each statement below, there is a set of words or phrases. Circle the letter next to the one word or phrase that best completes the sentence.

1. By 500 B.C., Darius ruled the whole civilized world west of central India with the exception of
    a) Egypt
    b) Israel
    c) Greece and Carthage
    d) all of the above
    e) none of the above

2. The most important city-state in Greece, and the one which met the Persian threat, was
    a) Athens
    b) Carthage
    c) Crete
    d) Sparta

3. Leonidas asked for men in his army to come forward to hold off the Persians so that 7,000 Spartans could escape. The number of men who volunteered was
    a) 300
    b) 350
    c) 5,300
    d) none of the above

4. The government of Athens was a
    a) republic
    b) dictatorship
    c) pure democracy
    d) aristocracy

5. The Parthenon was built to honor
   a) Zeus
   b) Apollo
   c) Acropolis
   d) Athena

6. The study of existence is called
   a) religion
   b) metaphysics
   c) rationality
   d) none of the above

7. The great Greek philosopher who reasoned to the concept of an eternal God, or Uncaused Cause, was
   a) Socrates
   b) Plato
   c) Aristotle
   d) Hippocrates

8. The war between Athens and Sparta was known as the
   a) War of the City-States
   b) Peloponnesian War
   c) Battle of Chaeronea
   d) Athenian War

9. The first city Alexander founded was Alexandria in
   a) Greece
   b) Rome
   c) Babylon
   d) Egypt

10. After eight years away from home, Alexander's weary troops finally refused to continue when they were in
    a) Egypt
    b) Babylon
    c) Iran
    d) Tyre
    e) India

True/False

Directions: Circle the letter T if the statement is true or F if the statement is false.

1. T F The Persian Wars ended in decisive defeat of the Persian army by the Greeks.

2. T F Miltiades was unprepared to deal with the Persians.

3. T F Because a traitor revealed to Xerxes the hidden mountain pass, the Spartan army was defeated by Persia.

4. T F In a pure democracy, all citizens meet to make laws and set policy, with one of their number carrying out the policies until the next assembly.

5. T F Through their statues, Greek sculptors were the first artists on record to depict human beings realistically.

6. T F Philosophy uses reason and logic to study questions such as, "What is reality?"

7. T F Aristotle believed that God took an interest in man.

8. T F Greek philosophy was very important to God's plan for Christ's Church.

9. T F Alexander's army was the second army to march across the Gedrosian Desert.

10. T F Alexander succeeded in defeating Persia.

11. T F Alexander did not oppress the native Persian peoples or deny them their customs.

12. T F Alexander died in Babylon at 32 years of age.

13. T F Alexander united the East and West in Greek language and culture, opening up lines of communication and transportation, thus helping the eventual Church to spread throughout the world.

Matching

Directions: This list is made up of names of persons, groups, places and things. Each one corresponds to one of the lettered phrases below. In each blank, write the letter of the phrase that correctly identifies that person, group, place or thing.

1. ___ Bardiya, son of Cyrus

2. ___ Darius the Great

3. ___ Miltiades

4. ___ Xerxes

5. ___ Pericles

6. ___ Sophocles

7. ___ Parmenides

8. ___ Socratic method

9. ___ Plato

10. ___ phalanx

11. ___ Companions

12. ___ scythe chariot

13. ___ Alexandria-the-Farthest

A) the best of Alexander's
   cavalry troops
B) Socrates' pupil
C) "the lie"
D) questions and answers
E) Persian weapon
   of war

F) Greek playwright
G) commander of Athenian
   forces
H) Alexander's main
   military formation
I) a city almost to the
   borders of China

J) Son of Darius
K) ruler of Athens
   during the Golden Age
L) Persian King
M) founder of Metaphysics

Mini-Essay Question:
(Extra credit—4 points.)

How did God use the Persian Wars to prepare indirectly for the coming of Christ?

Personal Opinion:

Name an important or interesting fact that you learned in this chapter. How could this fact affect your life?

Perfect Score: 100
(Each Question is worth 2 points.)

Score: _____

Completion

Directions: Complete and make each statement true and accurate by writing one or more words on each blank line.

1. The checkerboard fighting groups of the Romans were called _____ .

2. Rome won the allegiance of people they conquered by granting them Roman _____ .

3. The _____ conducted foreign policy, raised armies and kept peace and order within Rome.

4. The plebeians were protected from magistrates' oppressive laws by the _____ .

5. The Roman moral code was based on _____ .

6. The _____ Wars were those between Rome and Carthage.

7. The Romans took control of _____ , and defeated the naval power of the world at that time.

8. The 20-year-old _____ rejuvenated the remnants of the Roman army when it had been almost conquered by Hannibal, by urging all to swear by their blade not to desert Rome.

9. After conquering Carthage, the Romans sowed _____ in the earth to make it uninhabitable.

10. Antiochus' fury at _____ the Roman drove him to religious persecution against the Jewish people.

11. Antiochus and his pagans tried to destroy the faith of the Jewish people and change them from _____ (worshipers of the one true God) into _____ (worshipers of many false gods).

12. The _____ war of 91 to 88 B.C. was civil disorder at its highest in Rome as the Romans fought the other Italians they ruled.

13. The three-man rule of Caesar, Pompey and Crassus was called the

_____ .

14. One of the greatest contributions of Rome to the world was the development of

Natural Law _____ .

Multiple Choice

Directions: After each statement below, there is a set of words or phrases. Circle the letter next to the one word or phrase that best completes the sentence.

1. When they became independent from the Etruscans, the Romans set up a form of government known as
   a) pure democracy
   b) republic
   c) monarchy
   d) dictatorship

2. The number of independent classes of magistrates in Rome was
   a) one
   b) two
   c) three
   d) four
   e) five

3. The two most important magistrates in the Roman government were the
   a) tribunes and senators
   b) consuls and tribunes
   c) senators and plebians
   d) tribunes and patricians
   e) plebians and senators

4. The animal which Antiochus ordered the Jews to sacrifice in order to mock their religion was the
   a) lamb
   b) goat
   c) boar
   d) pig

5. Judas Machabeus used all of the following in his battles against the Greeks except
        a) meeting in open battle
        b) hit and run raids
        c) ambushes
        d) sabotage

6. The Romans became the rulers of the Jewish people in 63 B.C. when Palestine was annexed to the Roman Empire by General
        a) Sulla
        b) Pompey
        c) Mithridates
        d) Marius

7. The First Triumvirate consisted of
        a) Caesar, Crassus, Pompey
        b) Marius, Sulla, Caesar
        c) Marcus, Lepidus, Mark Antony, Octavian
        d) Mark Antony, Octavian, Crassus

8. The Roman ruler who was assassinated on March 15 (the Ides of March) of 44 B.C. was
        a) Julius Caesar
        b) Mark Antony
        c) Octavian
        d. Sulla

9. The spread of Roman culture into western and northern Europe happened especially through Caesar's conquest of
        a) Gaul
        b) Palestine
        c) Carthage
        d) none of the above

10. The great Roman ruler who ushered in a period of peace and prosperity in the last years B.C. was
        a) Julius Caesar
        b) Cicero
        c) Caesar Augustus
        d) Mark Antony

True/False

Directions: Circle the letter T if the statement is true or F if the statement is false.

1.   T   F   In a Pyrrhic victory, the winning side loses few men.

2.   T   F   Veto power was held by the magistrates in the Roman government.

3.   T   F   The religion of the Romans was a real advantage to their society.

4.   T   F   Child sacrifice to the god Moloch was common in Carthage.

5.   T   F   The Roman strategy against Hannibal is studied in military colleges.

6.   T   F   Rome always refused to negotiate with an enemy who was in arms on her territory.

7.   T   F   Hannibal was defeated by Scipio in the Second Punic War.

8.   T   F   The five sons of Mathathias were known as the Machabees because of the nickname given to John.

9.   T   F   Mathathias resisted the blasphemous sacrifice in Modein and inspired others to do so as well.

10.   T   F   Because of the heroism and perseverance of the Machabees, the Jews were independent from 141 B.C. to 63 B.C.

11.   T   F   After ordering Caesar to stop at the Rubicon, Pompey uttered the famous cry, "The die is cast!"

12.   T   F   Mark Antony deserted the critical battle against him near Greece because of his preoccupation with Cleopatra.

13.   T   F   Caesar Augustus was able to bring order to Rome.

Matching

Directions: This list is made up of names of persons, groups, places and things. Each one corresponds to one of the lettered phrases below. In each blank, write the letter of the phrase that correctly identifies that person, group, place or thing.

1. ___ King Pyrrhus

2. ___ legion

3. ___ magistrates

4. ___ Patricians

5. ___ Plebeians

6. ___ natural law

7. ___ honesty

8. ___ Delenda est Carthago

9. ___ Hannibal Barca

10. ___ Fabius the Delayer

11. ___ Machabees

12. ___ Julius Caesar

13. ___ Augustus

A) a Roman fighting unit
B) common people

C) Carthage must be destroyed

D) five brothers, sons of Mathathias

E) a natural virtue
F) launched the Second
   Punic War
G) god-like
H) men in authority

I) dictator
J) noblemen of Rome
K) excellent strategist
L) moral principles known
   through natural reason

M) ruler of Greece-
   Macedon

Mini-Essay Question:
(Extra credit—4 points.)

List the 4 contributions of Rome to the world which played an important role in God's plan for the redemption of the human race.

Personal Opinion:

Name an important or interesting fact that you learned in this chapter. How could this fact affect your life?

Supplemental Reading

Johnson, Hannan, Dominica. *Bible History*. TAN.

Perfect Score: 100
(Each Question is worth 2 points.)

Score: _____

Completion

Directions: Complete and make each statement true and accurate by writing one or more words on each blank line.

1. The _____ is the primary source of our information about Christ as a historical figure.

2. The first test of a historical document is its _____ in time to the events it describes.

3. There were _____ chief sects of Jews.

4. The story of the birth of Christ told in the Gospels is known as the _____ Narratives.

5. John the Baptist baptized Jesus in the _____ River.

6. One of the greatest sources of controversy between Jesus and the Pharisees was His assumption of the divine power to give and modify the _____ .

7. The cure of the man with the withered hand dispels the argument by some that Christ cured only people with illnesses which were _____ caused.

8. Opponents of Christianity also seek _____ explanations for some of Christ's miracles.

9. When Christ raised Lazarus from the dead, he had already been dead for _____ days. There can be no doubt that he was really dead and that he really came back to life.

10. There are _____ main theories which try to disprove the Resurrection.

11. The soldiers pierced Christ's _____ with a lance to make sure he was dead.

12. Christ's body was placed on a long piece of _____ folded length-wise over His body.

13. The Shroud confirms the Gospel accounts of the Passion and shows two coins over

the eyes which were minted only by _____ in Palestine between October of 28 A.D. and October of 31 A.D.

14. The Shroud indirectly confirms the _____ because only if the body in the Shroud miraculously passed out of it would the Shroud and its image

have been _____ .

Multiple Choice

Directions: After each statement below, there is a set of words or phrases. Circle the letter next to the one word or phrase that best completes the sentence.

1. Which of the following are tests for historical reliability?
   a) The documents are based on eyewitness accounts.
   b) There is corroboration by external, independent testimony.
   c) The accounts are not contradicted by anyone at the time.
   d) all of the above

2. The sect of Jews who retreated to the desert to await the Messiah were the
   a) Pharisees
   b) Sadducees
   c) Essenes
   d) Zealots

3. The birth of Christ is told in the first chapters of the Gospels of
   a) Matthew and Mark
   b) Matthew and Luke
   c) Mark and Luke
   d) John and Luke
   e) none of the above

4. The powers thought by the Jews to belong to God alone included
   a) the power to forgive sins
   b) the power to give and to change the Law
   c) the power to judge
   d. a. and c. only
   e) all of the above

5. Christ stated to the Jews that the Judge of all men would be
    a) Himself
    b) God the Father
    c) God the Holy Ghost
    d) all of the above

6. The traditional penalty for blasphemy was
    a) crucifying
    b) stoning
    c) flogging
    d) none of the above

7. The clear evidence that Jesus was God was
    a) His teaching
    b) His disposition
    c) His miracles
    d) none of the above

8. For doubters of Christianity, the miracles that are hardest to dispute are those in which
    a) Christ cured people
    b) Christ multiplied food
    c) Christ raised people from the dead
    d) none of the above

9. Among the women who came to the tomb to embalm the body of Jesus were
    a) Salome
    b) Mary, the mother of James
    c) Mary Magdalene
    d) a. and b. only
    e) all of the above

10. According to St. Paul, the risen Christ appeared to this number of people:
    a) 200
    b) 300
    c) 400
    d) 500
    e) none of the above

True/False

Directions: Circle the letter T if the statement is true or F if the statement is false.

1.   T   F   By using the birth of Christ as a measuring point for determining all dates, we acknowledge that the Incarnation is the most important event in history.

2.   T   F   The Gospels are historically reliable documents.

3.   T   F   The Jewish people were an easy province for the Romans to rule.

4.   T   F   Because Herod was essentially cruel, he refused to help the Jews with building projects such as the rebuilding of the Temple in Jerusalem.

5.   T   F   The Pharisees helped reduce the confusion among the people as to the meaning of the Law of Moses.

6.   T   F   The birth of Christ is true and can be confirmed by several sets of evidence.

7.   T   F   Herod Antipas was as cruel as his father.

8.   T   F   Jesus never explicitly claimed to be equal to God.

9.   T   F   Jesus revealed from the beginning of His ministry that He was God.

10. T   F   Mass hypnotism could explain the 12 baskets of bread left over after Jesus preformed the miracle of the loaves.

11. T   F   The story the guards spread of the Apostles stealing Jesus' body while they slept is still circulated today.

12. T   F   After the Resurrection, the Apostles refused to believe Mary Magdalene when she told them that she had seen Jesus.

13. T   F   The Apostles' testimony is all the more credible because they were so difficult to convince.

Matching

Directions: This list is made up of names of persons, groups, places and things. Each one corresponds to one of the lettered phrases below. In each blank, write the letter of the phrase that correctly identifies that person, group, place or thing.

1. ___   The Incarnation

2. ___   Josephus

3. ___   Herod the Great

4. ___   sect

5. ___   Pontius Pilate

6. ___   John the Baptist

7. ___   blasphemy

8. ___   I Am

9. ___   Sanhedrin

10. ___   Holy Shroud

11. ___   conspiracy theory

12. ___   hallucination theory

13. ___   Thomas

A) prophet who urged repentance in preparation for the Messiah
B) Hebrew name for God
C) the birth of Christ
D) claiming to be equal with God

E) Apostles saw a vision of Christ
F) division
G) said: "My Lord and My God."
H) burial cloth of Jesus
I) Client King

J) Apostles and others stole Christ's body
K) a Romanized Jewish historian
L) Procurator (Roman governor)
M) Jewish court

Mini-Essay Question:
(Extra credit—4 points.)

Some people use the 1988 Carbon 14 test to try to disprove the authenticity of the Shroud, saying it is a medieval forgery. Give two possible reasons why the Carbon 14 test could have yielded incorrect results.

Personal Opinion:

Name an important or interesting fact that you learned in this chapter. How could this fact affect your life?

Supplemental Reading

Johnson, Hannan, Dominica. *Bible History*. TAN.

Perfect Score: 100
(Each Question is worth 2 points.)

Score: _____

Completion

Directions: Complete and make each statement true and accurate by writing one or more words on each blank line.

1. In Matthew 16, Christ gives Simon the name _____ because he will be the foundation stone of the Church.

2. Peter and the other Apostles brought the message of Christianity first to the

   _____ .

3. Saul was present at the stoning of the first Christian martyr,

   _____ ; Saul was converted while he was on a journey to

   _____ .

4. Saul was to be the Apostle to the _____ .

5. James the Lesser remained in _____ to become its bishop.

6. According to the most reliable traditions, the Apostle Jude went to

   _____ , while Thomas went to _____ to preach the Gospel.

7. Jude brought the Shroud to _____ to cure King Abgar, and then established Christianity there.

8. When Jude brought the Shroud to King Abgar, folded and decorated, it showed the

   Holy _____ of Jesus.

9. The Romans thought Jesus' name was _____ .

10. To shift the blame from himself, Nero blamed the _____ for the fire of July 18, 64.

11. Paul, as a Roman citizen, was killed not by crucifixion but by

    _____ .

12. 69 A.D. was known as the "year of the _____ emperors."

13. After a miraculously failed attempt to kill him, John was exiled to the island of _____ in the Mediterranean where he wrote the Book of _____ .

14. Three important themes for the first century A.D. are: the growth and spread of the Church, the decline of _____ and the destruction of the _____ .

Multiple Choice

Directions: After each statement below, there is a set of words or phrases. Circle the letter next to the one word or phrase that best completes the sentence.

1. The Pharisee, Saul, was converted on the way to
    a) Damascus
    b) Palestine
    c) Athens
    d) Crete
    e) none of the above

2. The second persecution of the Christians was launched by
    a) The Pharisees
    b) King Herod Agrippa
    c) Emperor Claudius
    d) all of the above

3. Christian traditions tell of hundreds of cures and thousands of Baptisms at the community Thomas founded in
    a) Taxila
    b) Mylapore
    c) Malabar
    d) Mesopotamia

4. The descendants of the Christian community Thomas founded, which lasted over 1,000 years, are known as the
    a) Taxila Christians
    b) Mylapore Christians
    c) Malabar community
    d) Thomas Christians

5. The Shroud was hidden during the persecutions of Christians and was not rediscovered until an earthquake uncovered it inside the city gates of Edessa in this century:
   a) third
   b) fourth
   c) fifth
   d) sixth

6. Paul made missionary journeys to all the following except
   a) the Middle East
   b) India
   c) Greece
   d) Asia Minor

7. The accounts of Paul's journeys, recorded in the Acts of the Apostles, were written by
   a) himself
   b) St. Matthew
   c) St. Luke
   d) St. John

8. The Church's first council, called by Peter, met in 50 A.D. in
   a) Jerusalem
   b) Rome
   c) Edessa
   d) Greece

9. The Christian martyrs endured which of the following at Nero's Circus?
   a) being fed to wild beasts
   b) acting as murder victims in plays
   c) being soaked in oil
   d) being set on fire to serve as torches
   e) all of the above

10. The Roman army which responded to Zealot uprisings by conquering Jerusalem without mercy and destroying the Temple in 70 A.D. was led by
    a) Vespasian
    b) Titus
    c) Domitian
    d) Vitellius

True/False

Directions: Circle the letter T if the statement is true or F if the statement is false.

1.　T　F　It was common for a Jewish person to have Roman citizenship.

2.   T   F   Saul's new name, Paul, reflected his mission.

3.   T   F   Half of the Apostles went beyond the boundaries of the Roman Empire in trying to carry the Gospel to the ends of the world as Jesus had commanded.

4.   T   F   Paul used his letters to communities to continue teaching Christian doctrine and to help settle controversies arising in the communities after he left.

5.   T   F   Peter decided that Gentiles should be required to obey the Mosaic Law as the Law had not yet passed away.

6.   T   F   Paul was stranded on the island of Crete while on his way to Rome for trial.

7.   T   F   Total power can destroy those who possess it.

8.   T   F   Claudius died of natural causes.

9.   T   F   Nero was an extremely popular emperor.

10.   T   F   Christ prophesied that Peter would be crucified.

11.   T   F   The martyrdom of the Apostles fulfilled Christ's prophecy that "not one stone would be left upon another."

12.   T   F   The foundation of the west wall of the Temple, The Wailing Wall, was the site of weeping for Jews, who could no longer go to Jerusalem except once every four years.

13.   T   F   The letter from Pope Clement to the Corinthians proves that the Pope in Rome was regarded as having authority over the whole Church within the first century after Christ died.

Matching

Directions: This list is made up of names of persons, groups, places and things. Each one corresponds to one of the lettered phrases below. In each blank, write the letter of the phrase that correctly identifies that person, group, place or thing.

1. ___ Cenacle

2. ___ Pentecost Sunday

3. ___ Peter

4. ___ The Pope

5. ___ St. Stephen

6. ___ Gentiles

7. ___ James the Greater

8. ___ Caligula

9. ___ Nero

10. ___ Linus

11. ___ Vespasian

12. ___ Domitian

13. ___ Clement

A) non-Jews
B) first Apostle martyred
C) first Christian martyr
D) insane Roman ruler
E) upper room where the Apostles and the Blessed Mother waited for the Holy Spirit

F) paranoid ruler, persecuted Christians
G) a name that means "rock"
H) practical Roman ruler for 10 years
I) second Pope, successor to Peter

J) birthday of the Church
K) fourth Pope (reigned from 92-101)
L) Emperor who is said to have "fiddled while Rome burned"
M) head of the Church

Mini-Essay Question:
(Extra credit—4 points.)
Why was it necessary to locate the headquarters of the Church in Rome?

Personal Opinion:
Name an important or interesting fact that you learned in this chapter. How could this fact affect your life?

Supplemental Reading

Johnson, Hannan and Dominica. *The Story of the Church*. TAN.

Fr. John Laux. *Church History*. TAN.

Mary Fabyan Windeatt. *St. Paul the Apostle*. TAN.

Rev. D. I. Lanslots. *The Primitive Church—The Church in the Days of the Apostles*. TAN.

Fr. Vittorio Guerrera. *The Shroud of Turin: A Case for Authenticity*. TAN.

Perfect Score: 100
(Each Question is worth 2 points.)

Score: _____

Completion

Directions: Complete and make each statement true and accurate by writing one or more words on each blank line.

1. After Commodus died, there were _____ emperors in 90 years.

2. Emperor Valerian believed a superstition that the disasters of Rome were caused by the anger of the gods at the _____ .

3. St. Sixtus and the four deacons were _____ , which means they were witnesses.

4. Diocletian moved his capital to _____ in Asia Minor.

5. Diocletian suffered a psychological _____ , perhaps caused by guilt over ordering the persecution of Christians.

6. Although Diocletian ordered it, _____ and his mother _____ were largely responsible for the Great Persecution of Christians.

7. Constantine escaped Galerius and rode _____ miles on horse back to reach his father, Constantius.

8. Galerius' body was eaten away by an _____ .

9. Constantine saw a vision of a _____ in the sky.

10. Chi and Rho are the first two letters of the word _____ in Greek.

11. The _____ Bridge collapsed with Maxentius and his army when they crossed the Tiber, and Maxentius died in the mud.

12. The Edict of Milan is also known as the Edict of _____ .

13. The Edict rendered the empire officially _____ toward religion.

14. A society based upon laws reflecting the laws of God and Christian principles is

known as _____ .

Multiple Choice

Directions: After each statement below, there is a set of words or phrases. Circle the letter next to the one word or phrase that best completes the sentence.

1. Beginning around the year 96, a series of emperors brought peace and order to Rome. They are known as
   - a) the Good Emperors
   - b) the Great Emperors
   - c) the Talented Emperors
   - d) the Four Emperors

2. The emperors who were adopted and chosen to succeed peacefully include all of the following except
   - a) Trajan
   - b) Hadrian
   - c) Domitian
   - d) Marcus Aurelius

3. The decline of Rome included all of the following except
   - a) the decline of moral standards
   - b) the increase of population
   - c) the rising of prices and taxes
   - d) secret rituals involving mutilation

4. To restore order to Rome, Diocletian
   - a) established a sound currency
   - b) eliminated special privileges
   - c) appointed qualified men to important positions in local governments and the army
   - d) a. and c. only
   - e) all of the above

5. The priestess and mother of Galerius who taught her son to hate Christians was
   - a) Helena
   - b) Romula
   - c) Nervina
   - d) none of the above

6. The decree to persecute was not enforced in Gaul and Britain, which were under the authority of
   a) Severus
   b) Daia
   c) Constantius
   d) Commodus

7. Galerius appointed as Caesar:
   a) Constantine
   b) Daia
   c) Severus
   d) b. and c. only
   e) all of the above

8. Upon assuming power, Constantine and other powerful men met and discussed various questions including
   a) ordering the slaughter of enemies, as was customary
   b) religious freedom
   c) deposing the current Pope
   d) a. and c. only
   e) all of the above

9. Constantine modified Roman laws to include all of the following changes except
   a) promotion of gladiatorial fights
   b) protection of widows and orphans
   c) abolishing of crucifixion
   d) Sunday becoming a festival day

10. Constantine's mother, who went to the Holy Land and found the Cross on which Christ had died, was
    a) Helena
    b) Romula
    c) Nervina
    d) none of the above

True/False

Directions: Circle the letter T if the statement is true or F if the statement is false.

1.   T   F   Christianity against Rome was like Elias against the 450 priests of Baal in the Old Testament because both beat tremendous odds.

2.   T   F   The Colosseum was an important symbol of the spiritual health of Rome.

3.   T   F   The Good Emperors did not persecute Christians.

4.　T　F　Commodus continued to persecute Christians just like his father.

5.　T　F　A Pope may resign, but may not be deposed, because no one on earth has higher authority than the Vicar of Christ.

6.　T　F　Hippolytus finally realized his wrongs, and he repented and urged his followers to obey the true Pope.

7.　T　F　The papacy was vacant for almost a year because the Roman clergy feared electing another Pope while Decius lived.

8.　T　F　Diocletian's policy as emperor was to rule by violence and bloodshed.

9.　T　F　The Great Persecution, which began in 304 A.D., can be called the strongest effort in history to wipe out Christianity.

10.　T　F　Galerius continued to persecute Christians right up until the day he died of the horrible disease which afflicted his body.

11.　T　F　Constantine was in a weak military position against Maxentius and he knew it.

12.　T　F　The Latin words, "In hoc signo vinces," which Constantine saw in his vision, mean "In this sign you will conquer."

13.　T　F　The Edict of Milan allowed all people, including Christians, to observe their faith.

Matching

Directions: This list is made up of names of persons, groups, places and things. Each one corresponds to one of the lettered phrases below. In each blank, write the letter of the phrase that correctly identifies that person, group, place or thing.

1. ___ Nerva

2. ___ Trajan

3. ___ Commodus

4. ___ Praetorian Guard

5. ___ Calixtus

6. ___ Hippolytus

7. ___ Pontian

8. ___ Pope Fabian

9. ___ Sixtus II

10. ___ Galerius

11. ___ Constantius

12. ___ Saxa Rubra

13. ___ Cataphracti

A) insane son of Marcus Aurelius

B) first anti-pope; only one to be a saint

C) Pope while Valerian was emperor; martyr

D) heavily armed cavalry
E) helped assassinate Domitian
F) Red Rocks (Battle of the Milvian Bridge)
G) first Pope to resign his office
H) Pope in 217 who had been a slave laborer in the mines
I) Maximian's Caesar
J) Nerva's chosen successor
K) Diocletian's Caesar
L) the emperor's personal army
M) first person ordered by Decius to be martyred

Mini-Essay Question:
(Extra credit—4 points.)

What did Constantine do to the Roman laws, and of what is he considered the founder?

Personal Opinion:

Name an important or interesting fact that you learned in this chapter. How could this fact affect your life?

Supplemental Reading

Abbot Giuseppe Ricciotti. *The Age of Martyrs: Christianity from Diocletian (284) to Constantine (337)*. TAN.

Fr. A. J. O'Reilly. *The Martyrs of the Coliseum*. TAN.

CHRIST THE KING, LORD OF HISTORY — WORKBOOK

Perfect Score: 100
(Each Question is worth 2 points.)

Score: _____

Completion

Directions: Complete and make each statement true and accurate by writing one or more words on each blank line.

1. From 330 to 1453, _____ was the most important city in the world.

2. With the founding of Constantinople, the center of power shifted from Rome to the

   _____ .

3. In the debate during the Council of Nicaea, the arguments finally settled on the

   question of whether Christ was one in _____ with the Father.

4. The _____ is a summary of the most important teachings of Christianity which came out of the Council at Nicaea.

5. Pope _____ refused to support Arianism and was exiled and imprisoned.

6. The Pope, the ordinary people, and one bishop, _____ , stood

   firm against the Arian heresy.

7. Julian the _____ hated all Christians and wanted to restore paganism.

8. The Temple in Jerusalem has never been rebuilt; it is no longer needed due to

   the new and eternal _____ of the _____
   in the Catholic Church.

9. The preaching of St. _____ was important in the conversion of St. Augustine.

10. Conversions to the Christian Faith (such as Augustine's) come through

    _____ , which God may give because of the prayers of others.

11. The Council in _____ declared that Mary was indeed the Mother of God: *Theotokos*.

12. Nestorius claimed that Christ's humanity was merely a _____ which God put on, and that Mary bore that only.

13. Pope Leo the Great wrote the _____ of Leo in which he taught that Christ was one divine Person possessing two complete and perfect natures, divine and human.

14. _____ , the wife of Emperor Justinian, tried in every way to further the monophysite heresy.

Multiple Choice

Directions: After each statement below, there is a set of words or phrases. Circle the letter next to the one word or phrase that best completes the sentence.

1. After the founding of Constantinople, the Roman Empire started to become less Roman and more Greek or
        a) Jewish
        b) barbarian
        c) Hellenistic
        d) none of the above

2. The eastern empire became known as the
        a) Byzantine Empire
        b) Hellenistic Empire
        c) Grecian Empire
        d) Alexandrian Empire

3. The Bishop of Alexandria who played a crucial role in saving the True Faith from Arianism was
        a) Anthony of Egypt
        b) Athanasius
        c) Eusebius
        d) Arsenius

4. The Formulary of Sirmium that was so unmistakably Arian that even under torture Pope Liberius never signed it was the
        a) first
        b) second
        c) third
        d) none of the above

5. Athanasius wrote
        a) *History of the Arians*
        b) *On the Incarnation*
        c) *Life of St. Justin, Martyr*
        d) a. and b. only
        e) all of the above

6. The Fathers of the Church include
        a) St. Jerome
        b) St. John Chrysostom
        c) St. Augustine
        d) St. Ambrose of Milan
        e) all of the above

7. Before becoming a Christian, St. Augustine had been a
        a) Manichean
        b) Arian
        c) Monophysite
        d) Nestorian

8. The Nestorian heresy denies:
        a) that the Son always existed
        b) that Christ was truly a man
        c) that Mary is the Mother of God
        d) none of the above

9. The Council of Ephesus, which declared that Mary was the Mother of God, was led by
        a) Eusebius
        b) Augustine
        c) Ambrose
        d) Cyril of Alexandria

10. The anti-pope who became a validly elected Pope and then unexpectedly informed Empress Theodosia that he had decided to support true Catholic doctrine was
        a) Agapetus
        b) Anthimius
        c) Silverius
        d) Vigilius

True/False

Directions: Circle the letter T if the statement is true or F if the statement is false.

1.   T   F   Arianism states that the Son of God did not always exist; that because He was created by God, there was a time when He was not.

2.   T   F   The poor and uneducated liked Arianism because it made sense to them.

3.   T   F   Athanasius was accused of murder and of using a magic ritual.

4.   T   F   Constantine's ordering of Athanasius to be exiled to Trier is an example of Constans-papism, the attempt by the emperor to control the Church.

5.   T   F   So many mysterious things intervened when Julian was attempting to rebuild the Temple in Jerusalem that he was forced to abandon his plan.

6.   T   F   Athanasius went into hiding five times in his life.

7.   T   F   Manicheans believed that equally powerful principles of good and evil war within the universe.

8.   T   F   The first book Augustine read after hearing, "Take up and read" was the Gospel of St. John.

9.   T   F   After 7,000 defenseless people had been killed by order of Theodosius, Ambrose excommunicated Theodosius and insisted that public penance be done before he could again receive the Eucharist.

10.   T   F   Monophysitism denies Christ's divinity, while Nestorianism denies His humanity.

11.   T   F   Pope Leo condemned the council led by Dioscorus and the Monophysites as false, and it is known as the Flawed Council of Ephesus.

12.   T   F   Vigilius was an anti-pope who later became a validly elected Pope.

13.   T   F   After 10 years of exile and confinement, Vigilius finally gave in and died on the way home.

Matching

Directions: This list is made up of names of persons, groups, places and things. Each one corresponds to one of the lettered phrases below. In each blank, write the letter of the phrase that correctly identifies that person, group, place or thing.

1. ___ Constantinople

2. ___ Byzantium

3. ___ heresy

4. ___ Arianism

5. ___ Orthodoxy

6. ___ Anthony of Egypt

7. ___ Arius

8. ___ Constantius

9. ___ Augustine

10. ___ Theodosius

11. ___ Caesaro-papism

12. ___ St. Ambrose

13. ___ Theotokos

A) true doctrine
B) hermit saint
C) Emperor controls the Church
D) Istanbul, Turkey
E) sole ruler of Empire by 350
F) Mother of God

G) false doctrine
H) rhetorician
I) Emperor of Eastern half of Empire
J) Eastern Empire
K) confronted Emperor Theodosius
L) first great heresy

M) heretical deacon who preached in Alexandria

Mini-Essay Question:
(Extra credit—4 points.)

St. Cyril and the Council of Ephesus upheld that Mary deserves the title Mother of God because of what reason?

Personal Opinion:

Name an important or interesting fact that you learned in this chapter. How could this fact affect your life?

Supplemental Reading

Abbot Giuseppe Ricciotti. *Julian the Apostate*. TAN.

F. A. Forbes. *St. Athanasius*. TAN.

F. A. Forbes. *St. Monica*. TAN.

| **11** | **THE BARBARIANS AND THE CHURCH** | Text Pages 118-131 |

Perfect Score: 100
(Each Question is worth 2 points.)

Score: _____

Completion

Directions: Complete and make each statement true and accurate by writing one or more words on each blank line.

1. The ultimate solution to Rome's problems with decay and corruption was

   _____ .

2. The Battle of Adrianople in 378 was won by the _____ and marked the first permanent breach of Rome's frontier.

3. Pope _____ the Great intervened for the people with the Huns and the Vandals.

4. While Europe suffered through the Dark Ages, Ireland gloried in its

   _____ .

5. Colmcille's anger resulted in a war between Tirconnail and Diarmuid known

   as the "War of the _____ ."

6. St. _____ established monasteries all over Scotland.

7. The writings of the Irish monk, St. _____ , spoke of amazing voyages in a leather boat to lands west.

8. Ireland's holy saints founded many schools to which men from

   _____ and the continent of _____ came to study.

9. The monasteries preserved civilization during the Dark Ages. Here

   monks lived an ordered life of prayer, _____ and

   _____ .

10. The very fact that Arthur's grave was desecrated in England during the Protestant

    Revolt is proof that he was known as a _____ king.

11. A Catholic _____ is primarily responsible for the conversions of the Visigoths (in Spain) and the Franks (in France).

12. With the conversion of _____ to Catholicism, Spain became a Catholic nation.

13. Pope St. Gregory the Great fed the hungry people of _____ with the surplus of crops grown on Church property.

14. St. Augustine of _____ baptized King Ethelbert and 10,000 other Angles.

Multiple Choice

Directions: After each statement below, there is a set of words or phrases. Circle the letter next to the one word or phrase that best completes the sentence.

1. All of the following were barbarians who lived on the borders of Rome except
    a) the Huns
    b) the Goths
    c) the Visigoths
    d) the Vandals

2. The barbarians could never conquer the Byzantine Empire because of the superb location of
    a) Rome
    b) Kildaire
    c) Monte Cassino
    d) Constantinople

3. The Dark Ages lasted from approximately
    a) 300-600
    b) 450-1050
    c) 450-650
    d) 800-1000

4. This country was never a part of the Roman Empire:
    a) England
    b) Ireland
    c) Spain
    d) France

5. All of Ireland was Catholic within this many years after St. Patrick's coming:
    a) 25 years
    b) 50 years
    c) 75 years
    d) 100 years

6. Ireland's excellent schools drew students from Europe and England to study which of the following:
        a) theology, philosophy, law and logic
        b) geography, history and astronomy
        c) mathematics, grammar, music and art
        d) b. and c. only
        e) all of the above

7. Following the Benedictine Rule, the monks who enter the monastery promise to do all of the following except
        a) take daily recreation
        b) recite the Divine Office
        c) work
        d) study

8. King Clovis was baptized in Rheims Cathedral by St. Remi on Christmas Day of
        a) 396
        b) 496
        c) 596
        d) 696

9. Spain became Catholic some time after his martyrdom:
        a) Clovis
        b) Leovigild
        c) Reccared
        d) Hermenigild

10. On one of the prayer pilgrimages with Pope Gregory the Great, the plague stopped after a vision was seen of
        a) St. Gabriel the Archangel
        b) St. Raphael the Archangel
        c) St. Michael the Archangel
        d) none of the above

True/False

Directions: Circle the letter T if the statement is true or F if the statement is false.

1.   T F   When the Goths, under Alaric, invaded Rome and sacked it in 410, this was only the second time in its history that it had been conquered.

2.   T F   After the talk with Pope Leo, Attila tried to attack Rome.

3.   T F   The Byzantines vigorously tried to re-establish the empire, but were unable.

4.   T   F   The Dark Ages were called such because civilization, order and culture were overshadowed by the barbaric law of the sword.

5.   T   F   The conversion of Ireland to Catholicism was very rapid and peaceful.

6.   T   F   Colmcille wanted to convert as many pagans as people who died in the war that he had caused.

7.   T   F   The monks of Iona practiced a black martyrdom (a life of penance) since they could not offer a martyrdom of blood.

8.   T   F   Printing presses assisted the monks in Ireland in making their printing works of art.

9.   T   F   The purpose of the Benedictine Rule, which is still followed in monasteries today, is "that in all things God shall be glorified."

10. T   F   King Arthur's army prevented the Saxons from invading Britain, thereby preserving some civilization for almost a century.

11. T   F   St. Clotilde's example and prayers so affected her husband Clovis that he promised Jesus to be baptized if he should win the war against the Allemani.

12. T   F   Spain is known as the "Eldest Daughter of the Church."

13. T   F   Pope Gregory was responsible for the conversion of the Angles in England and the Lombards.

Matching

Directions: This list is made up of names of persons, groups, places and things. Each one corresponds to one of the lettered phrases below. In each blank, write the letter of the phrase that correctly identifies that person, group, place or thing.

1. ___ Emperor Valens

2. ___ Attila the Hun

3. ___ Pope Leo the Great

4. ___ Romulus Augustus

5. ___ Druid priests

6. ___ St. Bridget

7. ___ Colmcille

8. ___ Diarmuid

9. ___ Iona

10. ___ Aidan

11. ___ St. Benedict

12. ___ St. Columbanus

13. ___ Gregory the Great

A) Servant of the Servants of God

B) hostile to St. Patrick

C) Irish Saint who established monasteries in Europe

D) defeated in Battle of Adrianople

E) High King over all of
   Ireland
F) led a tribe of Orientals
   from Asia
G) "Father of Western
   Monasticism"

H) stood between the
   people of Rome and
   the barbarians
I) last Roman Emperor
   in the West (476)
J) Colmcille's missionary
   base in Scotland

K) Mary of the Gael
L) Also known as Columba
M) First Christian King
   of Scotland

Mini-Essay Question:
(Extra credit—4 points.)

How did the monasteries preserve civilization during the
Dark Ages?

Personal Opinion:

Name an important or interesting fact that you learned in
this chapter. How could this fact affect your life?

Supplemental Reading

St. Gregory the Great. *The Life of St. Benedict* (booklet). TAN.

Perfect Score: 100
(Each Question is worth 2 points.)

Score: _____

Completion

Directions: Complete and make each statement true and accurate by writing one or more words on each blank line.

1. _____ was located on the Tigris River and was the capital of the Persians.

2. The _____ is the book of Mohammed's ideas in which he preaches six doctrines.

3. The name of Mohammed's religion is _____ , while a follower of the religion is called a _____ .

4. People feared Mohammed's strong _____ and therefore his religion spread rapidly.

5. The Moslems swept through all of the civilized world and were stopped only _____ times.

6. Pelayo said: "Our hope is in _____ ; this little mountain will be the salvation of _____ and of the Gothic people; the loving kindness of Christ will free us from the multitude."

7. As a tribute to the enemy they could not defeat, the Moslems called all westerners _____ for centuries afterwards.

8. The Pope's decision to look to the West, rather than to the old Eastern Roman Empire, really freed the Church from the corruptions and confusions of _____ .

9. Pepin promised to defend Rome against the _____ .

10. The Donation of Pepin was land which later became the _____ .

11. Charlemagne believed that it was only through their _____ that the Saxons would be able to live peacefully.

12. The _____ Age during the last quarter of the eighth century in France is so named in honor of Charlemagne, who brought peace.

13. Because Charlemagne was the first Roman Emperor in the West since 476, and because his empire was based firmly on Christianity, his title was

_____ Roman Emperor.

14. While Constantine is the Founder of Christendom, Charlemagne is the

_____ of Christendom.

Multiple Choice

Directions: After each statement below, there is a set of words or phrases. Circle the letter next to the one word or phrase that best completes the sentence.

1. The following are all tenets of Mohammed's religion except
   a) war against infidels is praiseworthy
   b) Abraham is the greatest prophet
   c) revenge is permitted
   d) paradise is filled with material pleasures

2. The Battle of Yarmuk (636), the Moslems' first major victory, was fought against the
   a) Byzantines
   b) Persians
   c) Egyptians
   d) Indians

3. All the lands conquered by the Moslems then remain so today except
   a) Russia
   b) North Africa
   c) Afghanistan
   d) Spain

4. The Moslems were stopped at all of the following except
   a) Constantinople
   b) Covadonga
   c) Ctesiphon
   d) Tours

5. Moslems succeeded because of
   a) good cavalry troops
   b) inducements offered to people to convert
   c) death penalty for apostasy
   d) a. and c. only
   e) all of the above

6. The West's only hope against the Moslems for peace, order and culture rested in the
   - a) Byzantines
   - b) Spaniards
   - c) Franks
   - d) Saxons

7. When Pepin died, Charlemagne became ruler of all the Frankish lands, which roughly included all the following modern-day lands except
   - a) France
   - b) eastern Germany
   - c) Switzerland
   - d) Belgium
   - e) the Netherlands

8. Pope Leo III crowned Charlemagne the Holy Roman Emperor on Christmas Day of
   - a) 600 A.D.
   - b) 700 A.D.
   - c) 800 A.D.
   - d) 900 A.D.

9. Having a Holy Roman Emperor did which of the following:
   - a) limit the king's power
   - b) protect the Church
   - c) unite the people under one spiritual head, the Pope
   - d) b. and c. only
   - e) all of the above

10. The notion of the Holy Roman Emperor as the particular protector of the Pope and the Faith in Europe endured until which century:
   - a) 18th
   - b) 19th
   - c) 20th
   - d) none of the above

True/False

Directions: Circle the letter T if the statement is true or F if the statement is false.

1. T F The Persians were ruthless in their destruction of Jerusalem, demolishing every church and killing and enslaving 95,000 people.

2. T F The Feast of the Triumph of the Cross is September 14 in memory of Heraclius' march into Jerusalem to restore the relics of the True Cross.

3.   T   F   Mohammed accepted the Trinity as he proclaimed that there was one God, "Allah."

4.   T   F   The tribes in Arabia clearly understood Christianity and rejected it.

5.   T   F   The new religion from Mohammed only served to intensify the old divisions and hatreds among the Arab tribes.

6.   T   F   Apostasy is now common among Moslems since the death penalty is rarely invoked.

7.   T   F   The "thirty barbarians perched on a rock" who the Moslem general dismissed with contempt were the beginning of the "salvation of Spain."

8.   T   F   Only 100 years after Mohammed died, the Moslems controlled most of the civilized world.

9.   T   F   Much of the Arabs' religious zeal in fighting came from the belief that death in battle against infidels led to immediate entrance into paradise.

10.   T   F   Because of all the territory they conquered, the Moslems united the East and West.

11.   T   F   Pepin's son Carloman became known as Charlemagne.

12.   T   F   The Song of Roland is about Rolands's successful battle at Roncesvalles.

13.   T   F   The Byzantines were able to defend Constantinople from the Moslems with the invention of Greek fire.

Matching

Directions: This list is made up of names of persons, groups, places and things. Each one corresponds to one of the lettered phrases below. In each blank, write the letter of the phrase that correctly identifies that person, group, place or thing.

1. ___ Heraclius

2. ___ infidels

3. ___ Hegira

4. ___ Abu Bakr

5. ___ Caliph Omar

6. ___ Mogul Empire

7. ___ Pelayo

8. ___ Covadonga

9. ___ Martel

10. ___ King Pepin

11. ___ Woden

12. ___ Alcuin

13. ___ Charlemagne

A) flight of Mohammed to Medina
B) Spanish King who fought Moslems
C) hailed as savior of Christian civilization
D) "The Hammer"
E) monk who established schools
F) anointed King of Franks by Pope Stephen II
G) non-Moslems
H) Charles the Great
I) replaced the Harappan civilization
J) ordered devouring of the Christians
K) battle which liberated Spain from Moslems
L) pagan god of the Saxons
M) Mohammed's successor

Mini-Essay Question: Identify and describe the Carolingian Age in France.
(Extra credit—4 points.)

Personal Opinion: Name an important or interesting fact that you learned in this chapter. How could this fact affect your life?

13 THE FOUNDATION OF A NEW CIVILIZATION

Perfect Score: 100
(Each Question is worth 2 points.)

Score: _____

Completion

Directions: Complete and make each statement true and accurate by writing one or more words on each blank line.

1. The 9th and 10th centuries (approximately 814-1050) marked the end of the

   _____ .

2. Louis the Pious had _____ sons.

3. The Treaty of _____ (843) marked the beginning of the modern idea of nations.

4. The Treaty divided the Holy Roman Empire into three parts: _____ in the west, _____ in the east and Lotharingia in the middle.

5. Whereas other barbarians settled the lands they conquered, Viking raiding parties were made up of _____ only, who returned to their homes after looting and pillaging.

6. The power of God to make a difference through one person is clearly seen in King _____ the Great, who defeated the Danes at Ethandune in 878.

7. The nation of _____ can trace its beginning to that battle at Ethandune.

8. During the 900's, the exchange of labor for protection which developed in France, Germany and England was called _____ .

9. In the 10th century, the German kingdom of _____ gradually grew to be the strongest force in Europe.

10. The Synod of the _____ led by Stephen dug up Pope Formosus' body to judge and condemn him.

11. In his travels to monasteries to reform them, St. _____ met the resistance with the words, "I come peacefully—to hurt no one, injure no one, but that I may correct those who are not living according to [the Benedictine] Rule."

12. St. Cyril translated the liturgy and Scriptures into _____ to convert that people, while St. Methodius carried Christianity to the

_____ with a picture of the Last Judgment.

13. The promise of papal infallibility in the Catholic Church refers specifically to the

Church's teaching of _____ and _____ .

14. After General John Curcuas and his army brought the miraculous portrait of

Christ back to _____ , it was found to be a shroud—the burial cloth of Christ.

Multiple Choice

Directions: After each statement below, there is a set of words or phrases. Circle the letter next to the one word or phrase that best completes the sentence.

1. During 814-1050, all of the following happened except
   a) the decline and reappearance of the Holy Roman Emperor
   b) freedom from barbarian invasions
   c) the feudal system emerged
   d) difficulties of the papacy and the Church

2. Louis the Pious' sons were
   a) Charles the Fat and Lothair
   b) Lothair, Louis the German and Charles the Fat
   c) Lothair, Charles the Bald and Louis the German
   d) none of the above

3. Scandinavia includes all of the following except
   a) Ireland
   b) Norway
   c) Sweden
   d) Denmark

4. The family founder who led the Franks as the Carolingian dynasty died out was
   a) King Alfred
   b) Robert the Strong-armed
   c) Brian Boru
   d) Otto the Great

5. The French dynasty of Capetians lasted until which century:
   a) 14th
   b) 15th
   c) 16th
   d) 17th
   e) none of the above

6. The Viking invasions touched which country the least:
   a) France
   b) England
   c) Ireland
   d) Germany
   e) none of the above

7. After it was re-established, the Holy Roman Empire endured from 962 until
   a) 1536
   b) 1626
   c) 1716
   d) 1806
   e) none of the above

8. The Cluny monk who was Pope between 999-1003 and reformed the Church just as the Cluny saints had reformed the monasteries was
   a) Berno
   b) Sylvester II
   c) Odo
   d) Stephen

9. The person responsible for furthering Christianity in Denmark and all of Scandinavia was
   a) Canute the Great
   b) King Harold Blue Tooth
   c) Sweyn Fork Beard
   d) King Harold Fine Hair

10. The patron saint of Norway who fought paganism with English missionaries was
    a) King Harold Fine Hair
    b) Haakon the Good
    c) King Olaf II
    d) none of the above

True/False

Directions: Circle the letter T if the statement is true or F if the statement is false.

1.   T   F   Lothair became the Holy Roman Emperor because he was the strongest ruler among his brothers.

2.   T   F   Louis the Pious had a commanding personality, as did his father Charlemagne.

3.   T   F   Dividing the Empire so the sons of Louis the Pious would not fight resulted in peace, which strengthened the Empire.

4.   T   F   Charles the Fat was unworthy of Charlemagne's crown and was deposed in 887.

5.   T   F   Charles the Fat assisted Count Eudes in fighting the Vikings.

6.   T   F   The alternation of the title of King of Munster between the Desmond line and the Thomond line was harmonious.

7.   T   F   The laborers who worked the land of the knights who protected them were called fealtists.

8.   T   F   In the feudal system, the higher levels in society protected those lower down.

9.   T   F   In 962 the Pope re-established the Holy Roman Empire by crowning Otto the Great.

10.   T   F   Thanks to Stephen, who received a royal crown from the Pope in the year 1000, Hungary became Christian.

11.   T   F   G. K. Chesterton, the great Catholic writer, wrote the "Ballad of the White Horse" about Otto's victory at Lechfield.

12.   T   F   The century before the re-establishment of the Holy Roman Empire saw grave problems in the papacy, such as immorality and incompetence, as well as in the rest of the Church, with Church offices being bought and bishops taking bribes.

13.   T   F   Although there have been Popes who were great sinners, none of the Popes during the dark night of the papacy taught heresy.

Matching

Directions: This list is made up of names of persons, groups, places and things. Each one corresponds to one of the lettered phrases below. In each blank, write the letter of the phrase that correctly identifies that person, group, place or thing.

1. ___ Louis the Pious   6. ___ Capetians

2. ___ Lombardy   7. ___ Brian Boru

3. ___ Charles the Fat   8. ___ fief

4. ___ Danes   9. ___ fealty

5. ___ Ethandune   10. ___ Otto the Great

11. ___ Adelaide

13. ___ Olga

12. ___ Duke of Aquitaine

A) named after Count Eudes' descendent
B) founder of monastery at Cluny, France
C) northern Italy
D) mother of King Vladimir, who converted Russia
E) piece of land owned by knights or barons

F) King of Saxons; restored Holy Roman Empire
G) son of Charlemagne, succeeded him as king
H) Otto's holy wife, now a saint
I) Norsemen from Denmark

J) High King; first ruler of a united Ireland
K) loyalty and service
L) Louis the German's son; King in 881
M) site of King Alfred's victory

Mini-Essay Question: How did Brian Boru make a new golden age for his country?
(Extra credit—4 points.)

Personal Opinion: Name an important or interesting fact that you learned in this chapter. How could this fact affect your life?

Perfect Score: 100
(Each Question is worth 2 points.)

Score: _____

Completion

Directions: Complete and make each statement true and accurate by writing one or more words on each blank line.

1. The Dark Ages were brought to an end by the reform of the Church, the revival of

   the _____ , and the peace and economic revival resulting from

   the _____ .

2. With the conversion of the _____ in the fourteenth century, the Church encompassed every European people, so that by the year

   _____ , virtually every European was a baptized Catholic.

3. Through the synods and reform of dioceses, Pope Leo and Hildebrand

   fought the evils of _____ and violation of the law of priestly

   _____ .

4. Pope Blessed _____ is responsible for convoking the Council of

   _____ in November of 1095, which called the First Crusade.

5. The knights who fought in the Crusade wanted to free the Holy Land from the

   _____ and rescue Byzantium at the same time.

6. On July 15, 1099 the city of _____ was taken by the Crusaders despite great obstacles.

7. Soon after the conquest of Jerusalem, a new religious community was

   organized, called the _____ or _____ ,
   who dedicated themselves to God, cared for the sick and fought in the service of the Church.

8. The Second Crusade, although preached by _____ , was fraught with problems and accomplished little.

9. Pope Innocent III (1198-1216) re-established _____ in Rome while extending political power.

10. Those involved in the Sack of _____ were excommunicated by Pope Innocent III, but the relationship between Rome and the Greek Orthodox Church was destroyed.

11. Of the two groups attracted to the Albigensian heresy, the _____ were those who lived a highly ascetic life, while the second group used the heresy as a _____ freely.

12. St. Dominic first established an order of nuns to counteract the Albigensians' influence on women; next he established his Order of _____ , or Dominicans. Then he established the _____ Order Dominicans for lay people.

13. At the Battle of Muret, _____ , who was outnumbered forty to one, won an impressive victory and checked the political power of the Albigensians.

14. Because they were the most educated men in the Church, the Dominicans were put in charge of the _____ , a court used to try heretics.

Multiple Choice

Directions: After each statement below, there is a set of words or phrases. Circle the letter next to the one word or phrase that best completes the sentence.

1. All are true of the Greek and Russian Orthodox Churches today except
   a) they teach basically the same doctrines as the Catholic Church
   b) they have valid sacraments
   c) they accept the authority of the Holy Father
   d) they are descendants of the schismatic churches in the Greek Schism

2. The Greek Schism took place in
   a) 1054
   b) 1154
   c) 1254
   d) 1354

3. The Cluny-educated Benedictine monk who was the dominant figure in Rome twenty years before his election, and who served as Pope from 1073 to 1085, was
        a) Victor II
        b) Stephen X
        c) Nicholas II
        d) Gregory VII

4. All were dominant figures in the First Crusade except
        a) Bohemond
        b) Godfrey de Bouillon
        c) Raymond of Toulouse
        d) Henry IV
        e) a. and d.

5. The new order founded by St. Bernard of Clairvaux was the
        a) Cistercians
        b) Capuchins
        c) Carthusians
        d) Knights Templar

6. The brilliant battle against Saladin which showed the tactical skill of Baldwin, the Leper King, was the Battle of
        a) Damascus
        b) Ramleh
        c) Arsuf
        d) Jaffa

7. King James of England was forced to sign the Magna Carta at
        a) Aquitaine
        b) Runnymede
        c) Damascus
        d) Chalus-Chabrol

8. Pope Innocent III is responsible for
        a) mediating between Hungarian royalty
        b) arbitrating the crown of Sweden
        c) restoring ecclesiastical discipline in Poland
        d) a. and c. only
        e) all of the above

9. The Albigensian heresy taught all of the following except
        a) an evil principle created all material things
        b) suicide was commendable
        c) earth was a place of punishment in preparation for Hell
        d) there was no Resurrection of Jesus or of human bodies
        e) procreation and childbearing were to be avoided

10. The custom of the Nativity Scene is credited to:
   a) St. Thomas Becket
   b) St. Bernard of Clairvaux
   c) St. Francis of Assisi
   d) St. Dominic

True/False

Directions: Circle the letter T if the statement is true or F if the statement is false.

1. T F William Duke of Normandy took the throne through the Norman Conquest in 1066 and established the Norman dynasty of competent rulers in England.

2. T F Clerical incompetence is a term referring to priests who do not remain celibate.

3. T F Henry IV was using investiture of his own men as Bishops and expanded that to include the bestowal of symbols of spiritual authority as well, thus bringing him into the Investiture controversy with Pope Gregory.

4. T F The Sack of Constantinople and of Jerusalem were not immoral since the Crusades were a just war.

5. T F Raymond of Toulouse and Godfrey de Bouillon were humble men; they refused to wear a crown of gold.

6. T F His consecration as Archbishop of Canterbury on June 10, 1162, began a dramatic change from worldliness to holiness for Thomas Becket.

7. T F Thomas Becket's clash with King Henry II was really about the Church's moral authority over secular rulers.

8. T F An interdict placed on a country by the Pope means that that country gets less financial support from him.

9. T F It took Thomas Becket's death to move King Henry's heart to finally grant the Church the rights over which he had previously opposed Thomas.

10. T F Saladin was not very impressed with Richard the Lion-Heart but nonetheless agreed to a three-year truce.

11. T F The Magna Carta guaranteed the rights of the poor against the noblemen.

12.   T   F   The Catholic missionaries before Dominic had not made much headway combating the Albigensians because they were too highly educated and lived too austerely for these simple people.

13.   T   F   The habit of the Franciscan order is the same grey beggar's robe and cord which St. Francis wore.

Matching

Directions: This list is made up of names of persons, groups, places and things. Each one corresponds to one of the lettered phrases below. In each blank, write the letter of the phrase that correctly identifies that person, group, place or thing.

1. ___ Pope Gregory VII

2. ___ Michael Cerularius

3. ___ Nicholas II

4. ___ Henry IV

5. ___ Godfrey de Bouillon

6. ___ Hospitallers

7. ___ Calixtus II

8. ___ St. Robert

9. ___ Baldwin IV, Leper

10. ___ Richard Lion-Heart

11. ___ Simon de Montfort

12. ___ Portiuncula chapel

13. ___ Franciscans

A) German Emperor who was excommunicated twice
B) took the title of Defender of the Holy Sepulcher
C) restored full Benedictine Rule at Citeaux
D) Pope who solved investiture problem
E) King of Jerusalem

F) Friars Minor (Little Brothers)
G) Hildebrand
H) son of King Henry II and Eleanor of Aquitaine
I) original home of the Friars Minor
J) Patriarch of Constantinople; led Greek Schism

K) military order; protectors of Holy Sepulcher
L) fought Albigensians with the sword
M) set up College of Cardinals which elects Pope

Mini-Essay Question:
(Extra credit—4 points.)

Give two reasons why the Christian nations of Europe were not the aggressors in the Crusades.

Personal Opinion:

Name an important or interesting fact that you learned in this chapter. How could this fact affect your life?

Supplemental Reading

Mary Fabyan Windeatt. *St. Dominic*. TAN.

Augusta Drane. *Life of St. Dominic*. TAN.

St. Bonaventure. *Life of St. Francis of Assisi*. TAN.

Hilaire Belloc. *The Crusades*. TAN.

<table>
<tr><td>**15**</td><td>**THE GREATEST
OF CENTURIES**</td><td>Text
Pages
182-200</td></tr>
</table>

Perfect Score: 100
(Each Question is worth 2 points.)

Score: _____

Completion

Directions: Complete and make each statement true and accurate by writing one or more words on each blank line.

1. King St. Louis _____ (number) ruled justly, supported the Pope, and fought the Moslems in Egypt.

2. The Holy Roman Emperor _____ was excommunicated by Pope Gregory IX when he proclaimed himself supreme over the Pope.

3. As a young child, the intellectual Thomas Aquinas pondered questions such as "What is _____ ?"

4. Thomas Aquinas showed the harmony of faith and _____ ; he demolished Siger of Brabant's idea of the "two _____ ."

5. _____ is the doctrine on the Eucharist developed by St. Thomas Aquinas which states that the substance of bread and wine ceases to exist and is replaced by the substance of the Body and Blood of Christ, while the appearances of bread and wine remain.

6. In the guilds, the apprentices became _____ who worked on their own. Eventually they could earn the title of _____ .

7. The code of Christian conduct for knights, the institution of _____ , promoted courage, honor, the protection of the weak and the defense of the Church.

8. Modern science had its beginnings during the High Middle Ages, especially with _____ and _____ , who learned to observe and experiment with nature.

9. The _____ refers to the 60-year period in which Rome was not the headquarters of the papacy; Rome was deserted in favor of Avignon, France.

10. The key issue of the Hundred Years' War was whether _____ would survive as a nation.

11. God used St. Joan of Arc to help France stay independent. This protected its

    _____ because, had England ruled France, 100 years later when England rejected the Church, France might have been lost too.

12. The Church's problems and the decline of the High Middle Ages included the Babylonian Captivity, the rise of nationalism and the bubonic plague, which is

    commonly called the _____ .

13. In _____ , the year of the fall of Constantinople to the Turks, the Roman Empire in the East finally fell.

14. The three Johns: John Carvajal (Cardinal), John Hunyadi and John Capistrano (Saint) fought Mohammed the Conqueror at Pope Calixtus III's urgent request and

    saved the country of _____ and Europe.

Multiple Choice

Directions: After each statement below, there is a set of words or phrases. Circle the letter next to the one word or phrase that best completes the sentence.

1. The summit of the High Middle Ages, called "the greatest of centuries," was which century:
   - a) 12th
   - b) 13th
   - c) 14th
   - d) 15th
   - e) None of the Above

2. King St. Louis IX of France spent time doing which of the following:
   - a) prayer and penance
   - b) feeding the poor and founding hospitals
   - c) fighting the Moslems
   - d) a. and b. only
   - e) all of the above

3. After writing about the Body of Christ, St. Thomas was granted
   - a) mystical visions
   - b) good health
   - c) a leadership role at the Council of Lyons
   - d) b. and c.
   - e) all of the above

4. The Cathedral at Chartres was an example of which type of architecture:
> a) Basilica
> b) Gothic
> c) Romanesque
> d) Roman

5. The two customs which the Church used to combat the violence of the feudal lords against each other were
> a) the Rule of God and the Truce of God
> b. the Peace of God and the Rule of God
> c) the Truce of God and the Peace of God
> d) none of the above

6. The Council which attempted to end the Great Schism but instead elected a second anti-pope and ended with three men claiming papal authority was held at
> a) Noyon
> b) Lyons
> c) Constance
> d) Pisa

7. The Great Schism was healed with the valid election of Pope
> a) Martin V
> b) Urban VI
> c) Gregory IX
> d) Gregory XII

8. Which war was a primary example of the rise of nationalism:
> a) the War between Hungary and the Turks
> b) the War between France and Hungary
> c) the Hundred Years War
> d) none of the above

9. St. Joan of Arc, at age 18, heard voices of all of the following except
> a) St. Anne
> b) St. Catherine
> c) St. Michael the Archangel
> d) St. Margaret

10. The ways in which the bubonic plague contributed to the decline of the Middle Ages included
> a) less trust in God, more bitterness
> b) clergymen who were not very holy
> c) drastic decrease in population
> d) a. and c. only
> d) all of the above

True/False

Directions: Circle the letter T if the statement is true or F if the statement is false.

1. T F Queen Blanche reunited all of the Albigensian provinces with France in 1229.

2. T F King Louis IX consecrated his whole life to the glory of God and sought to do good for his people and the Church.

3. T F Although Frederick II rejected Christian doctrine and tried to be supreme over the Pope, he still promoted peace in his lands.

4. T F When King St. Louis IX tried to recapture the Holy Land but was himself captured, Queen Blanche directed the army to defend Damietta so that he could bargain for freedom for himself and his men.

5. T F St. Thomas Aquinas was visited by the Virgin Mary, who tied a burning cord around his waist, so he would never be tempted against purity again.

6. T F The *Summa Contra Gentiles* defends Catholic doctrine, while the *Summa Theologica* defends the harmony between faith and reason.

7. T F The "two truths" doctrine that Siger of Brabant proposed in 1269 stated that even though rational truth and religious truth were two separate truths, they could not contradict each other.

8. T F The beauty of the Cathedral at Chartres reminded the people of their home in Heaven and how they would get there.

9. T F *Unam Sanctam*, issued in 1303 by Pope Boniface VIII, angered King Philip IV of France because it said the Church had the right to judge all things including the actions of kings.

10. T F Nationalism means that loyalty is shared equally between Church and government of the nation instead of loyalty to Church coming first.

11. T F It is estimated that 30% of Europeans died of the bubonic plague.

12. T F Pope Calixtus III fixed the celebration of the Feast of the Transfiguration on August 6 in thanksgiving for the victory of the three Johns against the Turks at Belgrade.

13. T F The Shroud is now the property of the Church.

Matching

Directions: This list is made up of names of persons, groups, places and things. Each one corresponds to one of the lettered phrases below. In each blank, write the letter of the phrase that correctly identifies that person, group, place or thing.

1. ___ Louis IX
2. ___ Queen Blanche
3. ___ Margaret of Provence
4. ___ Albert the Great
5. ___ Guilds
6. ___ Lancets
7. ___ Roses

8. ___ Roger Bacon
9. ___ Pope Clement V
10. ___ St. Bridget of Sweden
11. ___ St. Catherine of Siena
12. ___ Lauda Sion
13. ___ Geoffrey de Charney

A) tall stained glass windows
B) scientist, teacher of St. Thomas
C) Master of Normandy
D) Louis IX's mother; regent for a time
E) wrote *The Secrets of Art and Nature*
F) persuaded Gregory IX to leave Avignon
G) responsible for the Babylonian Captivity
H) groups of craftsmen
I) persuaded Pope Urban V to return to Rome
J) greatest King of the 13th century
K) St. Thomas Aquinas
L) Louis IX's wife/adviser, mother of 11
M) circular stained glass windows

Mini-Essay Question:
(Extra credit—4 points.)

What is the argument that St. Thomas Aquinas used to refute and settle the Manichean (Albigensian) heresy?

Personal Opinion:

Name an important or interesting fact that you learned in this chapter. How could this fact affect your life?

Supplemental Reading

F. A. Forbes. *St. Catherine of Siena*. TAN.

John Beevers. *St. Joan of Arc*. TAN.

Anonymous. *St. Thomas Aquinas* (booklet). TAN.

St. Bridget. *The Revelations of St. Bridget of Sweden*. TAN.

16

SPAIN BECOMES A GREAT POWER

Perfect Score: 100
(Each Question is worth 2 points.)

Score: _____

Completion

Directions: Complete and make each statement true and accurate by writing one or more words on each blank line.

1. The only small strip of land which remained in Christian hands after the Moslems conquered was in the _____ mountains, which Pelayo and his men had fought for at the Battle of Covadonga.

2. The winning back of Spain from the Moslems took 770 years (from 722-1492) and is known as the _____ .

3. _____ , known as El Cid Campeador, followed King Pelayo's and King Alfonso II's shining examples in helping to free Spain.

4. Even though the weak and jealous King _____ of Castile had exiled him, El Cid was faithful in returning when the King needed him.

5. Two results of the victory by King Alfonso VIII and Archbishop Rodrigo were that the quality of the _____ declined, and that the Castillian kings took over the rivers and _____ , allowing communication throughout Spain again.

6. Following King Alfonso VIII was King St. Ferdinand of Castile (1217-1252), who won back for Spain the major Moslem kingdom of _____ in 1236 and then _____ in 1248.

7. Alfonso the Fat launched an attack on behalf of the _____ , which was the first challenge which Ferdinand and Isabel faced.

8. Through her hard efforts at raising money and recruiting, Isabel created the _____ and Ferdinand trained it.

9. Isabel knew that once Spain was Christian again, it would be a leading power in _____ for the cause of _____ .

10. The _____ and _____ (falsely converted Jews and Moors) in high positions in Church and government were a real threat to the unity of Spain.

11. The court which Isabel set up to distinguish the faithful Christians from the traitors was called the _____ .

12. Those found guilty by this court were guilty of being traitors to the _____ and to the _____ .

13. Spain's _____ refers to the years of Ferdinand and Isabel's reign, when there were enormous advances in art, literature, culture and science.

14. Portugal opened up the _____ for Europe, but Spain opened up the _____ .

Multiple Choice

Directions: After each statement below, there is a set of words or phrases. Circle the letter next to the one word or phrase that best completes the sentence.

1. King Alfonso II did all of the following except
    a) regained Oviedo
    b) rebuilt the Church of the Twelve Apostles
    c) built the Shrine of Santiago de Campostella
    d) won against Yusuf ibn-Tashfin

2. The territory regained by Spain under Alfonso II included
    a) Navarra
    b) Leon and Castile
    c) Aragon
    d) b. and c. only
    e) all of the above

3. The Battle of Cuarte was fought for
    a) Leon
    b) Aragon
    c) Valencia
    d) none of the above

4. On July 16, 1212, the largest Spanish Christian army and the largest Moslem army ever assembled in Spain met at
    a) Valencia
    b) Las Navas de Tolosa
    c) Santiago de Campostella
    d) Sagrajas

5. At the battle on July 16, 1212, the Christians divided center, left and right with these in the center:
   a) King Alfonso VI and Archbishop Rodrigo
   b) King Alfonso VIII and Archbishop Rodrigo
   c) King Alfonso II and Rodrigo Diaz
   d) none of the above

6. By 1248, thanks to Pelayo, Alfonso II, Rodrigo Diaz, Alfonso VIII and King St. Ferdinand of Castile, the only land still left to be regained for Spain from the Moslems was
   a) Granada
   b) Cordoba
   c) Seville
   d) Valencia

7. The last Moslem ruler in Spain surrendered to Isabel and Ferdinand in
   a) 1292
   b) 1392
   c) 1492
   d) 1592

8. Ferdinand and Isabel are responsible for all of the following except
   a) discovering a sea route to India
   b) ending civil war and restoring order and justice in Spain
   c) completing the Reconquista
   d) reforming the Church in Spain

9. Scholars would come from all over Europe to study in Spain, the intellectual capital of the world, in the
   a) 14th Century
   b) 15th Century
   c) 16th Century
   d) 17th Century

10. Queen Isabel's title, *La Reina Catolica*, was bestowed on her by
   a) King Ferdinand
   b) King Henry IV
   c) the Pope
   d) the people

True/False

Directions: Circle the letter T if the statement is true or F if the statement is false.

1.   T   F   St. James the Apostle became the patron saint of the Reconquista after his bones were discovered at Campostella.

2.   T   F   During the fighting with the Moors, Archbishop Rodrigo thought the Christian troops would die, but King Alfonso VIII reassured him they would not only live, but conquer.

3.   T   F   After the death of King St. Ferdinand, Spain had even more problems from the Moslems.

4.   T   F   Ferdinand escaped King Henry's troops by disguising himself as a mule driver.

5.   T   F   The marriage of Isabel and Ferdinand is an example of a true love match and a genuine partnership.

6.   T   F   In order to re-establish order in Castile, Isabel and Ferdinand tried to stay at their castle as much as possible to see all of the people who came to them with grievances.

7.   T   F   Ferdinand and Isabel were able to reduce crime, violence and corruption while at the same time raising morality in Spain.

8.   T   F   When the last Moorish stronghold in Spain was taken at Cordoba, the silver cross was erected and the soldiers, King and Queen knelt in the dust to give thanks.

9.   T   F   Isabel reformed the Church by raising the education and moral standards of clergymen and stopping the selling of indulgences.

10.   T   F   One reason people use the Inquisition to attack Spain is that they resent the strong Catholic character of Spain.

11.   T   F   People accused of regular crimes in Spain pretended to be heretics so as to be tried by the Inquisition, because prisoners of the Inquisition were treated better.

12.   T   F   Despite the good intentions of its founders, the Spanish Inquisition increased the number of deaths caused later by the religious wars and the witchcraft hysteria.

13.   T   F   Columbus' deep faith convinced Isabel to support him and he sent a message of triumph to her despite a very difficult voyage home on the *Nina*.

Matching

Directions: This list is made up of names of persons, groups, places and things. Each one corresponds to one of the lettered phrases below. In each blank, write the letter of the phrase that correctly identifies that person, group, place or thing.

1. ___   King Alfonso II

2. ___   Santiago de Campostella

3. ___   El Cid Campeador

4. ___   King Henry IV

5. ___ Ferdinand of Aragon

6. ___ Santa Hermandad

7. ___ Boabdil

8. ___ Tomas de Torquemada

9. ___ Prince Henry
of Portugal

10. ___ India

11. ___ Portugal

12. ___ Spain

13. ___ La Reina Catolica

A) St. James in Field of the Star
B) local police force established by Ferdinand and Isabel
C) Dominican named Grand Inquisitor by Pope
D) source of spices
E) The Chaste
F) Catholic Queen
G) opened up the New World
H) half-brother to Isabel
I) opened up the East Indies to Europe
J) last Moslem ruler in Spain
K) The Navigator
L) Isabel's husband and King
M) lord or master, expert warrior

Mini-Essay Question:
(Extra credit—4 points.)
State the 3 major criticisms made against the Inquisition. Refute each.

Personal Opinion:
Name an important or interesting fact that you learned in this chapter. How could this fact affect your life?

Supplemental Reading

Willam Thomas Walsh. *Isabella of Spain—The Last Crusader*. TAN.

Willam Thomas Walsh. *Characters of the Inquisition*. TAN.

Perfect Score: 100
(Each Question is worth 2 points.)

Score: _____

Completion

Directions: Complete and make each statement true and accurate by writing one or more words on each blank line.

1. Renewed interest in the culture, art and ideas of _____ (ancient Greece and Rome) around the middle of the 14th century resulted in the Renaissance.

2. The philosophy that stressed human accomplishments and pride and confidence in the human mind is called _____ .

3. Christ chose the Apostle who denied Him to be the first _____ so that people would know He would protect the Church even when the Pope acted _____ .

4. Martin Luther taught that nothing we do has _____ , and that we cannot earn more _____ or become holier.

5. The removal of some or all of the punishment due to already forgiven sins by performing a good work or saying a prayer is an _____ .

6. The Catholic concept of _____ , in which all other Catholics on earth and the Saints in Heaven can help us to live a holier life, was also opposed by Luther and Calvin. They taught that no one could help another person spiritually; each person was alone.

7. The problems Charles V inherited at 20 years of age included the Protestant Revolt, the raids by the _____ , Francis I and the French trying to take over _____ , and the order needed in the New World.

8. The _____ family, to which Charles V belonged, understood the tremendous responsibilities of the Holy Roman Emperor; they were to wear the crown from 1483-1918.

9. Charles V ruled for _____ years; during that time he almost single-handedly held off the enemies of Christendom.

10. Charles V knew that if people followed Luther's rejection of authority over their individual consciences, this would eventually lead to _____ and the demise of the society.

11. The uprising of pro-Lutheran noblemen in 1522 known as the _____ War and the subsequent uprising by peasants in 1524 proved that the Lutherans wanted power, not just "freedom of conscience."

12. The _____ of April 19, 1529 by the Lutherans was their response to Ferdinand's Catholic decree at Speier and marked their being called Protestants.

13. When Charles abdicated in 1556, the imperial crown was passed on to his brother _____ , while his son _____ received the crowns of Spain and Burgundy.

14. In the painting of Charles V by the artist Titian, the imperial crown is cast aside and all of Charles' attention is on _____ .

Multiple Choice

Directions: After each statement below, there is a set of words or phrases. Circle the letter next to the one word or phrase that best completes the sentence.

1. Which of these weakened the Church during the Renaissance?
   a) nationalism
   b) humanism
   c) wealth and power
   d) a. and c. only
   e) all of the above

2. All were problems within the Church during the Renaissance except
   a) neglect of spiritual duties by bishops
   b) simony
   c) heresy
   d) priests leading immoral lives
   e) nepotism

3. Luther's document nailed to the church in Wittenberg, Germany on October 31, 1517 which called for a debate on indulgences was called the
        a) 95 Theses
        b) 59 Theses
        c) Thesis on Indulgences
        d) Theory on Indulgences

4. The scandal involving a bishop's debt to the Fugger's banking house resulted in the Church being falsely accused of
        a) buying indulgences
        b) selling indulgences
        c) granting indulgences
        d) keeping indulgences

5. The thought of more power and money (through the seizing of Church lands) led which group to support Luther against the Church:
        a) German peasants
        b) German businessmen
        c) German merchants
        d) German noblemen
        e) none of the above

6. Which of Calvin's doctrines states that man has no free will and that God has already pre-determined all of what man does, even his sins?
        a) total depravity
        b) predestination
        c) doctrine of the Elect
        d) none of the above

7. Which of the following is/are among the three enemies to Christendom which Charles V spent his life fighting as Holy Roman Emperor?
        a) the Lutherans
        b) the Turks
        c) Francis I, King of France
        d) all of the above

8. The document Charles V used to allow Protestants to practice their religion until a council could be called was
        a) the Interim of Augsburg
        b) the Peace of Augsburg
        c) the Peace of Nurnberg
        d) the Treaty of Cambrai

9. The decree permitting Protestants to keep the land they had seized was
>   a) the Interim of Augsburg
>   b) the Peace of Augsburg
>   c) the Peace of Nurnberg
>   d) the Treaty of Cambrai

10. Finally, in 1555, to stop the bloodshed, Charles V decreed that the religion of the nobleman ruling an area would be the religion of the people in
>   a) the Interim of Augsburg
>   b) the Peace of Augsburg
>   c) the Peace of Nurnberg
>   d) the Treaty of Cambrai

True/False

Directions: Circle the letter T if the statement is true or F if the statement is false.

1. T F The interest in Greek and Roman civilization was never harmful to Christian culture.

2. T F Because of the immoralities of Popes Alexander VI, Julius II, and Leo X, people lost faith in the papacy and began to think that Christ had abandoned the Catholic Church.

3. T F Martin Luther believed that his sins were very great but that God would forgive them and take them away.

4. T F Luther believed that God would not punish men for their sins if they had faith, and so they were to "sin on bravely."

5. T F Luther was excommunicated in 1520 by Pope Leo, who condemned 41 of his doctrines.

6. T F Calvin's doctrine of the Elect essentially denies that God wants all souls to be saved, since He has already chosen those He will damn.

7. T F Although Luther and Calvin revolted against existing spiritual authority, they advocated adherence to temporal authority.

8. T F Charles V, crowned Holy Roman Emperor just about 3 years after Luther began the revolt, was a very capable and just monarch who believed that God had given him the Empire as a sacred trust. He took this just as seriously as a religious vocation.

9. T F Charles issued the Edict of Worms to forbid people to protect Luther.

10. T F Charles urged Pope Clement VII to call a council to deal with the Lutheran crisis, but the Pope kept delaying.

11.   T   F   The Turkish sultan Saladin finally drove the Knights of St. John from Rhodes, and they withdrew to Malta.

12.   T   F   Pope Clement VII supported Charles against Francis I.

13.   T   F   Charles financed Ferdinand Majellan's voyage and tried to bring justice to the natives of the New World.

Matching

Directions: This list is made up of names of persons, groups, places and things. Each one corresponds to one of the lettered phrases below. In each blank, write the letter of the phrase that correctly identifies that person, group, place or thing.

1. ___ Renaissance

2. ___ Machiavelli

3. ___ Alexander VI

4. ___ John Calvin

5. ___ Geneva

6. ___ Puritans

7. ___ Romanists

8. ___ Charles V

9. ___ Rudolf I

10. ___ Francis I/France

11. ___ Diet of Worms

12. ___ Isabel of Portugal

13. ___ Maurice of Saxony

A) wrote *The Institutes of the Christian Religion*
B) meeting of leaders in 1521 regarding Luther's revolt
C) first Hapsburg to be Holy Roman Emperor (1273)
D) Calvinists who settled New England

E) developed theory— end (growth of power) justifies means (even if unjust)
F) Luther's word for the Catholic Church
G) where Calvin set up his ideal city-church
H) wife of Charles V
I) bought his election

J) failed to enforce Interim of Augsburg
K) rebirth
L) a Hapsburg; grandson of Maximillian I
M) traitor to Charles and Catholicism

Mini-Essay Question:
(Extra credit—4 points.)

Briefly explain how the actions of Luther and Calvin were not a "Reformation" but a Revolt.

Personal Opinion:

Name an important or interesting fact that you learned in this chapter. How could this fact affect your life?

Supplemental Reading

Hilaire Belloc. *Characters of the Reformation.* TAN.

Hilaire Belloc. *How the Reformation Happened.* TAN.

Msgr. Patrick F. O'Hare. *The Facts about Luther.* TAN.

Perfect Score: 100
(Each Question is worth 2 points.)

Score: _____

Completion

Directions: Complete and make each statement true and accurate by writing one or more words on each blank line.

1. The civil wars in England were fought between the _____ and

   _____ families for the throne of the insane King Henry VI.

2. When Richard of York was killed during the Battle of _____
   Field in 1485, Henry Tudor picked up the crown which had been hanging on

   a bush, unlawfully declared himself King, and began the _____
   dynasty.

3. A decree that two people had never really been married, that the marriage is

   invalid, is called an _____ .

4. _____ confiscated the monastery lands in 1536 and distributed
   them among his friends, who became wealthy and did not want the Church to
   return to power.

5. In 1552, Thomas Cranmer wrote the Book of _____ Prayer,
   which denied that the Mass was sacrificial and that the bread and wine were
   changed into the Body and Blood of Christ.

6. Because the _____ instituted by Cranmer looked in many
   ways like the Mass, it was years before the people understood that their religion
   was not Catholic anymore.

7. In her five-year reign (beginning when she was 37 years old),

   _____ did everything she could to restore Catholicism,
   including marrying Philip II, abolishing the Act of Supremacy and the Book of
   Common Prayer.

8. Foxe's Book of _____ , written five years after Mary Tudor's
   death, has unjustly marred her reputation throughout history.

9. The ordinary people obeyed Elizabeth, and Anglicanism became equated with

_____ .

10. Under Elizabeth I, anyone being reconciled to the Church was convicted of high

_____ and priests were executed as _____ .

11. As the brilliant Edmund Campion read the teachings of the Fathers of the Church,

he realized that the _____ position was wrong. When Elizabeth began repressing Catholics in Ireland in 1570, he went to the seminary

for Englishmen in _____ , Belgium to become a priest.

12. Edmund Campion hid in a " _____ hole" to escape

_____ , the professional priest-hunter whom he forgave and urged to go to Confession.

13. Mary Stuart was a member of the _____ family—one of the bravest, noblest and most dedicated Catholic families in France.

14. The _____ were forgeries upon which Mary Stuart was convicted in England (in a court that had no authority to convict her) of conspiring with James Bothwell to kill her second husband, Henry Darnley.

Multiple Choice

Directions: After each statement below, there is a set of words or phrases. Circle the letter next to the one word or phrase that best completes the sentence.

1. The civil wars in England between the York and Lancaster families for the throne of Henry VI were the
    a) War of the Lancasters and Yorks
    b) Wars of the Roses
    c) Hundred Years War
    d) none of the above

2. The man who was awarded the title "Defender of the Faith" because of his pamphlet *In Defense of the Seven Sacraments* was
    a) Henry VI
    b) Henry VII
    c) Henry VIII
    d) Sir Thomas More

3. In 1534, England formally went into schism, declaring Henry VIII head of the Church in England and Anne's children legitimate heirs to the throne, when Parliament passed the
   a) Act of Supremacy
   b) Oath of Supremacy
   c) Act of Legitimacy
   d) Oath of Legitimacy

4. Bishops and important citizens affirmed allegiance to Henry VIII as head of the Church in England (thus saving their lives) through the
   a) Act of Supremacy
   b) Oath of Supremacy
   c) Act of Legitimacy
   d) Oath of Legitimacy

5. Loyal northern English Catholics protested the confiscation of the monastery lands through the
   a) Uprising of Grace
   b) Uprising of Faith
   c) Pilgrimage of Grace
   d) Pilgrimage of Faith

6. Henry VIII's only living son, Edward, was born in 1537 to Henry's third wife,
   a) Anne Boleyn
   b) Anne of Cleves
   c) Catherine Howard
   d) Jane Seymour

7. The "Bloody Mary" legend written by Foxe in which Mary is falsely accused of "martyring" 273 people for their religious beliefs refers to
   a) Mary Tudor
   b) Mary Stuart
   c) Mary York
   d) Mary Lancaster

8. Henry VIII separated England from the Catholic Church, but Elizabeth furthered and finished the task during her reign of
   a) 15 years
   b) 25 years
   c) 35 years
   d) 45 years
   e) 55 years

9. The use of assassins and priest-hunters, the setting up of the first fully formed intelligence network in Europe, all for subverting the Church and promoting Protestantism, were accomplished by Elizabeth's secretary of state,

       a) Cardinal Wolsey
       b) Thomas Cromwell
       c) Thomas Cranmer
       d) Robert Cecil
       e) William Cecil

10. All of the following were true in Elizabethan England under "Good Queen Bess" except

       a) fines for non-attendance at Anglican services
       b) no public display of objects of devotion was allowed (this was only allowed in the home)
       c) Mass was illegal
       d) death after second refusal to take the Oath of Supremacy
       e) informers reported on priests and Catholic activity

True/False

Directions: Circle the letter T if the statement is true or F if the statement is false.

1.   T F   Thomas More (Henry VIII's chancellor) and Bishop John Fisher were martyred because they refused to take the Oath of Supremacy.

2.   T F   Cranmer tried to become wealthy by seizing Church lands.

3.   T F   The Pilgrimage of Grace by Catholics in northern England was the only serious opposition to Henry VIII's takeover of the English Church.

4.   T F   Anne Boleyn was the mother of Elizabeth.

5.   T F   Henry VIII executed all of his wives except his last one, Catherine Paar, who outlived him.

6.   T F   Thomas Cromwell won control of young Edward, heir of Henry VIII.

7.   T F   Cranmer was a heretic who replaced the Mass with a "communion service."

8.   T F   Both Henry VIII and Queen Elizabeth executed more people than Mary Tudor.

9.   T F   The rightful heir to Mary Tudor's throne was Elizabeth I, her half-sister.

10.   T   F   Although at Cecil's urging, Elizabeth restored the Act of Supremacy and Book of Common Prayer, she kept the existing bishops in office for continuity.

11.   T   F   St. Edmund Campion suffered in the Tower of London, was put on the rack, and then finally was martyred by beheading.

12.   T   F   After Mary Stuart's adviser David Rizzio was killed, she turned to James Bothwell, who ultimately abandoned her.

13.   T   F   During Elizabeth's reign, the rightful Queen would have been Mary Tudor.

Matching

Directions: This list is made up of names of persons, groups, places and things. Each one corresponds to one of the lettered phrases below. In each blank, write the letter of the phrase that correctly identifies that person, group, place or thing.

1. ___ Catherine of Aragon

2. ___ Cardinal Wolsey

3. ___ Cardinal Campeggio

4. ___ Thomas Cromwell

5. ___ Thomas Cranmer

6. ___ Robert Aske

7. ___ Anne of Cleves

8. ___ Mary Tudor

9. ___ Anglicans

10. ___ Margaret Clitherow

11. ___ Mary Stuart

12. ___ John Knox

13. ___ Seton clan

A) fought Protestants at Battle of Langside
B) members of the Church of England
C) led Pilgrimage of Grace to re-establish Catholic Church in England
D) Henry VIII's fourth wife
E) daughter of Isabel; first wife of Henry VIII
F) Queen of Scots; member of Guise family
G) politician, adviser to Henry VIII; wanted wealth
H) daughter of Henry VIII and Catherine of Aragon
I) Calvinist in Scotland; saw Mass as a disaster
J) Henry VIII's Chancellor; petitioned Rome for annulment
K) Legate to Pope Clement VII; ruled against Henry VIII
L) hid priests; was martyred under Elizabeth
M) Bishop, adviser to Henry; wanted power

Mini-Essay Question: Explain why the title, "Bloody Mary," is unfair to Mary Tudor.
(Extra credit—4 points.)

Personal Opinion: Name an important or interesting fact that you learned in this chapter. How could this fact affect your life?

Supplemental Reading

Rev. Dr. Nicolas Sander. *The Rise and Growth of the Anglican Schism*. (A 16th-century classic.) TAN.

William Cobbett. *History of the Protestant Reformation in England and Ireland*. (A 19th-century classic.) TAN.

Dr. Malcolm Brennan. *Martyrs of the English Reformation*. Angelus Press, Kansas City, MO.

19 THE CATHOLIC DEFENSE

Perfect Score: 100
(Each Question is worth 2 points.)

Score: _____

Completion

Directions: Complete and make each statement true and accurate by writing one or more words on each blank line.

1. The remains of _____ of Lyons and _____ of Tours were thrown into the Loire River by the Huguenots.

2. The term _____ describes the outrageous behavior of the Calvinist mob.

3. The only ruler who answered Pope St. Pius V's call for a new crusade against the Turks was _____ .

4. The _____ ordered the arrest and trial of men guilty of destroying churches, desecrating the Host and leading the rebellion against Philip II.

5. The _____ provided for the death penalty for all plotters against Elizabeth.

6. The struggle for power in France after the death of Charles IX is known as the _____ .

7. The country of _____ was saved for the Faith when Henri of Navarre switched religions for the fourth time.

8. The Irish clans of _____ and _____ fought English rule.

9. The Nine Years War strengthened the Faith of the _____ .

10. The country named for King Philip II is _____ .

11. In the _____ , French soldiers killed nearly 5,000 Huguenots, including women and children.

12. In the _____ , the Turks were stopped from overrunning Malta and Christian Europe.

CHAPTER 19 — THE CATHOLIC DEFENSE

13. Like his father, Philip II accepted responsibility of defending Christendom against

attacks of the _____ and the _____ .

14. The Duke of _____ , a strong Catholic and skilled military commander, was chosen by Philip II to lead the Spanish Armada.

Multiple Choice

Directions: After each statement below, there is a set of words or phrases. Circle the letter next to the one word or phrase that best completes the sentence.

1. Philip II had San Lorenzo del Escorial built in thanksgiving for this victory:
   - a) Spanish Armada
   - b) Nine Years War
   - c) Battle of San Quentin
   - d) none of the above

2. The Wars of Religion in France were begun by
   - a) Turks
   - b) Catholics
   - c) Huguenots
   - d) none of the above

3. In the Wars of Religion, atrocities were perpetrated such as
   - a) churches were devastated
   - b) priests and nuns were killed
   - c) tombs of saints were violated
   - d) a and c only
   - e) all of the above

4. The Calvinists called the execution of rebels Egmont and Hearne
   - a) the Council of Blood
   - b) the Babington Plot
   - c) the Revolt of the Beggars
   - d) the St. Bartholomew's Day Massacre

5. In gratitude to Our Lady for victory at the Battle of Lepanto, Pope St. Pius V declared that day, October 7,
   - a) Our Lady's Victory
   - b) Siege of Lepanto
   - c) Lepanto Victory
   - d) Feast of the Most Holy Rosary

6. Mary, Queen of Scots was falsely accused through a scheme known as the
      a) Act of Association
      b) Babington Plot
      c) Stuart letters
      d) Cecil's Revenge

7. The defeat of the Spanish Armada
      a) assured that Elizabeth would continue on the throne
      b) made England the greatest naval power in the world
      c) renewed Philip II's hopes of restoring English Catholicism
      d) a. and b. only
      e) all of the above

8. The Irish clans made an alliance against Elizabethan oppression and began the:
      a) Nine Years War
      b) War of the Three Henries
      c) Battle of Gembloux
      d) Flight of the Earls

9. The persecution of Catholic Irish leaders, which resulted in their transport to Europe, is known as the:
      a) Ulster Plantation
      b) Ulster Seizure
      c) Flight of the Earls
      d) Flight of the O'Donnell's

10. The Nine Years War indirectly resulted in which country being preserved Catholic:
      a) Spain
      b) Belgium
      c) Austria
      d) Holland

True/False

Directions: Circle the letter T if the statement is true or F if the statement is false.

1.   T   F   King Philip II and Robert Cecil were great adversaries.

2.   T   F   Catherine d' Medici was very obedient to the Church.

3.   T   F   The Siege of Malta resulted in victory for the Turks.

4.   T   F   The Revolt of the Beggars refers to actions of the noblemen in the Low countries.

5.   T   F   Philip II had his son Carlos arrested to prevent him from joining the Protestants.

| 6. | T | F | The Duke of Alba was a deeply dedicated Catholic. |

| 7. | T | F | Mary Stuart was tried fairly and found guilty of plotting Queen Elizabeth's overthrow. |

| 8. | T | F | The defeat of the Spanish Armada was accepted by Philip II as God's Will. |

| 9. | T | F | James I signed a lasting treaty with the Irish. |

| 10. | T | F | Queen Elizabeth died a peaceful death. |

| 11. | T | F | Red Hugh O'Donnell and Hugh O'Neil led the Irish to victory at the Battle of Yellow Ford—the worst disaster Elizabeth suffered in her reign. |

| 12. | T | F | The Guise family was Protestant. |

| 13. | T | F | Because of the Battle of Lepanto, the Turks never again attacked Christian Europe by sea. |

Matching

Directions: This list is made up of names of persons, groups, places and things. Each one corresponds to one of the lettered phrases below. In each blank, write the letter of the phrase that correctly identifies that person, group, place or thing.

1. ___ Philip II

2. ___ Henry II

3. ___ Isabel of Valois

4. ___ San Lorenzo del Escorial

5. ___ Francis II

6. ___ Suleiman

7. ___ Catherine d' Medici

8. ___ Duke of Guise

9. ___ La Valette

10. ___ Pope St. Pius V

11. ___ Huguenots

12. ___ Don Juan of Austria

13. ___ Medina Sidonia

A) monastery-palace near Madrid
B) Turkish ruler
C) King of France
D) Henry II's widow
E) Grand Master of the Knights

F) wife of Philip II
G) son of Henry II, ruler for a time
H) King of Spain (Charles V's son)
I) called for a Crusade

J) was shot by a poisoned bullet
K) military hero of Lepanto
L) commander of the Spanish Armada
M) French Calvinists

Mini-Essay Question: Summarize briefly what Catherine d' Medici did in order to
(Extra credit—4 points.) bear children and what her children suffered because of this.

Personal Opinion: Name an important or interesting fact that you learned in this chapter. How could this fact affect your life?

Supplemental Reading

William Thomas Walsh. *Philip II*. TAN.

Perfect Score: 100
(Each Question is worth 2 points.)

Score: _____

Completion

Directions: Complete and make each statement true and accurate by writing one or more words on each blank line.

1. In Catholic Church history, the 16th century is known as the Counter Reformation, or the _____ .

2. St. Ignatius' _____ took four weeks.

3. St. Ignatius of Loyola and his followers called themselves the Society of _____ ; they are also known as the _____ .

4. St. Ignatius' Society was organized like an _____ ; its members took a special vow of obedience to the _____ .

5. Besides reforming Church discipline, the Council of Trent _____ (stated the exact meaning of) Church doctrine.

6. The reforms of the Council of Trent were put into effect by Pope St. _____ , who was elected in 1566.

7. St. _____ carried out the reforms of the Council of Trent as Bishop of the diocese of Milan, Italy.

8. St. Teresa of Avila and St. John of the Cross reformed the _____ Order.

9. Within 30 days, _____ converted more Indians than the Portuguese had in 50 years.

10. Through his patience and care, Father Matteo Ricci opened up _____ , the most inaccessible country of his time, to Christianity.

11. _____ was the great missionary to India and Japan.

12. Catholics in _____ maintained the Catholic Faith without priests from the 17th to the 19th century.

13. After the Blessed Mother appeared at _____ and left her miraculous image on the cloak of a poor Indian, nearly the whole population of Mexico was converted in less than a century.

14. The Conquistador _____ destroyed the evil Aztec Empire of Mexico and ended its thousands of human sacrifices.

Multiple Choice

Directions: After each statement below, there is a set of words or phrases. Circle the letter next to the one word or phrase that best completes the sentence.

1. The Catholic Reformation happened during which century?
        a) 15th
        b) 16th
        c) 17th
        d) 18th

2. St. Ignatius spent ten months in prayer, penance, study and hospital work in:
        a) Montserrat
        b) Toledo
        c) Manresa
        d) Madrid

3. In 1518, St. Ignatius went to the greatest university in the world, that in
        a) Madrid
        b) Alcala
        c) Lyons
        d) Paris

4. Pope Paul III accomplished the following:
        a) he curbed indulgence abuses
        b) he required monks to live in parish rectories
        c) forbade enslavement of American Indians
        d) a. and c. only
        e) all of the above

5. St. Philip Neri was called the Apostle of
        a) Florence
        b) Italy
        c) Rome
        d) Assisi

6. By his efforts, St. Peter Canisius won back to the Church parts of
   a) France
   b) Belgium
   c) Switzerland
   d) Germany

7. All of the following were part of the Catholic Reformation except:
   a) Francis de Sales
   b) Henri Bourbon of Navarre
   c) Charles Borromeo
   d) Matteo Ricci

8. He was one of the original group of seven Jesuits:
   a) Francis Xavier
   b) Peter Canisius
   c) John of the Cross
   d) Philip Neri

9. The territory lost to the Church due to the Protestant Revolt was
   a) one-half
   b) one-fifth
   c) one-fourth
   d) one-third

10. All were Catholic Church doctrines defined by the Council of Trent except:
    a) baptism removes sins rather than just covering them up
    b) man is saved by faith alone
    c) by good works a man can merit an increase of grace
    d) grace is offered to all, not just to the Elect
    e) Purgatory exists
    f) indulgences may be granted

True/False

Directions: Circle the letter T if the statement is true or F if the statement is false.

1.   T   F   St. Ignatius and the Jesuits took a special vow of zeal.

2.   T   F   The Jesuits established schools and universities throughout Europe to train Catholics.

3.   T   F   During Elizabeth's reign, Jesuits were protected in England.

4.   T   F   Pope Paul III saw no need to call a council, so he delayed it time and again.

5.   T   F   Pope Pius V is now a saint.

6.   T   F   The Council of Trent reformed the Church by initiating several new Catholic doctrines.

7.   T   F   Thanks to St. Peter Canisius, Poland, which had become largely Protestant, returned to the Church.

8.   T   F   St. Peter Canisius set up oratories in Rome.

9.   T   F   Baroque was a style of art and architecture produced by the Catholic Reformation's optimism and devotion.

10.   T   F   By its missionary efforts, the Church showed how healthy it really was in the 16th century.

11.   T   F   Father Matteo made conversions among the Chinese by adopting their customs.

12.   T   F   The Society of Jesus is organized like an army, with firm displine, strict obedience and careful training.

13.   T   F   The Council of Trent allowed indulgences in return for contributions of money only in certain, limited circumstances.

Matching

Directions: This list is made up of names of persons, groups, places and things. Each one corresponds to one of the lettered phrases below. In each blank, write the letter of the phrase that correctly identifies that person, group, place or thing.

1. ___ Charles Borromeo

2. ___ Francis Xavier

3. ___ Matteo Ricci

4. ___ Bernini

5. ___ Jesuits

6. ___ Teresa of Avila

7. ___ Francis de Sales

8. ___ Pope Paul III

9. ___ John of the Cross

10. ___ Inigo Lopez

11. ___ Roberto di Nobili

12. ___ St. Pius V

13. ___ Catholic Reformation

A) Society of Jesus
B) reformed Carmelite Convents
C) converted Catholics from Calvinisim
D) St. Ignatius of Loyola
E) brought Catholicism to China

F) imprisoned by fellow Carmelites
G) Jesuit in Far East
H) reforming Bishop
I) Baroque artist
J) the first reforming Pope in the Catholic Reformation

K) carried out Council of Trent reforms
L) 16th century renewal of the Church
M) the Teacher of Reality

Mini-Essay Question: What did St. Ignatius and the Jesuits do that showed their
(Extra credit—4 points.) love of obedience? Contrast this with Martin Luther's actions.

Personal Opinion: Name an important or interesting fact that you learned in this chapter. How could this fact affect your life?

Supplemental Reading

F. A. Forbes. *St. Ignatius Loyola*. TAN.

F. A. Forbes. *St. Teresa of Avila*. TAN.

St. Ignatius Loyola. *Spiritual Exercises of St. Ignatius*. TAN.

Fr. V. J. Matthews. *St. Philip Neri—Apostle of Rome*. TAN.

St. Francis de Sales. *An Introduction to the Devout Life*. TAN.

Professor Robin Anderson. *St. Pius V*. TAN.

William Thomas Walsh. *St. Teresa of Avila*. TAN.

Perfect Score: 100
(Each Question is worth 2 points.)

Score: _____

Completion

Directions: Complete and make each statement true and accurate by writing one or more words on each blank line.

1. The _____ century saw a great expansion in scientific knowledge, with Newton, Harvey, Galileo and Copernicus making major contributions.

2. _____ is the belief that although God created the universe, He does not exercise providence over it nor does He care about individuals.

3. Then, even as now, theologians' views sometimes conflicted with the official teaching of the Church. Theological opinion does not represent the

   _____ or official teaching of the Roman Catholic Church.

4. With the quality of rulers of Spain and the Holy Roman Empire declining in the

   sixteenth and seventeenth centuries, the country of _____ rose to prominence.

5. Cardinal _____ (Louis XIII's chief minister), through the accomplishment of his two goals, was responsible for France emerging as the leading power in Europe.

6. The three-step plan he enacted to make Louis XIII all powerful in France

   included: 1) breaking the power of the _____ , 2) setting up

   a bureaucracy and 3) eliminating the influence of _____ .

7. A _____ is a large, complicated organization of government officials.

8. During Phase II of the Thirty Years War, Denmark intervened because the Danish

   Lutherans wanted to stop the powerful Catholic _____ .

9. When the _____ pirates stole Spanish silver and gold from the

New World, Olivares had to resort to direct _____ to carry on the Thirty Years War.

10. When his chief minister Cardinal _____ died, Louis XIV ruled as absolute monarch, fulfilling his desire to rule supreme.

11. Louis XIV did allow exploration of North America, and the French settled

_____ , which they called New France.

12. After studying with Descartes, _____ , Queen of Sweden (Gustavus Adolphus' daughter), sacrificed her throne to become a Catholic, so convinced was she that this was the True Church.

13. Because of King John Casimir's vow to honor Mary when Poland was liberated

from the Lutherans, Our Lady of _____ has been honored as Queen of Poland since 1660, when the treaty was signed.

14. The Battle of Zenta resulted in the Treaty of _____ which marked the end of Turkish attacks on Christian Europe.

Multiple Choice

Directions: After each statement below, there is a set of words or phrases. Circle the letter next to the one word or phrase that best completes the sentence.

1. When Copernicus published *Revolutions of the Celestial Orbs*, he advanced the theory of
        a) Geocentrism
        b) Heliocentrism
        c) Heterocentrism
        d) none of the above

2. The system of centralization of power for the King through bureaucracies is known as
        a) absolutism
        b) determinism
        c) deism
        d) none of the above

3. The achievement of Cardinal Richelieu's goal of making France all powerful came about through the
    a) Day of the Dupes
    b) Edict of Nantes
    c) Treaty of the Pyrenees
    d) Thirty Years War

4. When two Hapsburg governors in Prague were thrown out of the window by Bohemian Protestants, this became known as the
    a) restitution of Prague
    b) dethroning of Prague
    c) defenestration of Prague
    d) none of the above

5. The fighting of the Thirty Years War started because the Protestants wanted Ferdinand removed from office and replaced by
    a) Frederick of the Palatinate
    b) Frederick of Bohemia
    c) Gustavus Adolphus
    d) Louis XIII

6. The key battle of the Thirty Years War occurred early in the war, on November 8, 1620, when the Catholic general Tilly devastated the Lutheran army under Mansfeld in Bohemia in the
    a) Battle of Nordlingen
    b) Battle of the White Mountain
    c) Battle of the Pyrenees
    d) Battle of Zenta

7. In 1629, Ferdinand declared that the Protestants must give back all the Church property they had seized since the Peace of Augsburg in 1555. This declaration was the
    a) Edict of Nantes
    b) Edict of Restitution
    c) Treaty of Westphalia
    d) Treaty of the Pyrenees

8. The King known as "the Sun King" was
    a) Gustavus Adolphus
    b) Ferdinand of Bohemia
    c) Henry of Navarre
    d) Louis XIV

9. Our Lord revealed His Sacred Heart to St. Margaret Mary Alacoque and urged that Holy Communion be received frequently. This counteracted the concept that God was angry and man almost always unworthy to receive the Sacraments, that is,

      a) Jansenism
      b) Deism
      c) Determinism
      d) none of the above

10. The Thirty Years War ended with this important treaty, which marked the acceptance of a permanently split Christendom:

      a) Peace of Augsburg
      b) Treaty of Westphalia
      c) Treaty of Pyrenees
      d) Treaty of Carlowitz

True/False

Directions: Circle the letter T if the statement is true or F if the statement is false.

1. T   F   One result of the scientific revolution was intellectual pride, which led to Deism.

2. T   F   Determinism taught the concept of man's free will.

3   T   F   The Duke of Lerma succeeded in wrecking Spain's economy to the point that it was dependent on gold and silver from the New World to finance the wars Spain helped Christendom to fight.

4. T   F   Henry IV issued the Edict of Nantes in 1598, giving Protestants freedom of worship but limiting their political rights.

5. T   F   The Day of the Dupes refers to the day the siege at La Rochelle against the Huguenots began.

6. T   F   Under the Edict of Restitution issued by the Holy Roman Emperor Ferdinand, all Protestants were allowed freedom of worship.

7. T   F   Richelieu tried to strengthen the power of the Hapsburgs as a means of strengthening France's position.

8. T   F   Gustavus won a series of victories against the Spanish army because of his innovations in fighting, such as inventing a light cannon and training horsemen to ride at a gallop while shooting and using swords.

9. T   F   St. Margaret Mary Alacoque founded the Daughters of Charity, an order of nuns who serve the poor.

10.   T   F   St. Vincent de Paul warned that genuine conversion comes not by force but through love and good example.

11.   T   F   The Black Madonna (painting of Mary) is in a monastery in Vienna.

12.   T   F   After the Polish King, John Sobieski, won the battle against the Turks at Vienna, Pope Innocent declared September 12 the Feast of the Holy Name of Mary in thanksgiving for Our Lady's intercession.

13.   T   F   Eugene had to turn his attention from the Turks in order to fight in the War of the League of Augsburg against the French, thus keeping the Hapsburgs from defeating the Turks.

Matching

Directions: This list is made up of names of persons, groups, places and things. Each one corresponds to one of the lettered phrases below. In each blank, write the letter of the phrase that correctly identifies that person, group, place or thing.

1. ___ Isaac Newton

2. ___ William Harvey

3. ___ Robert Bellarmine

4. ___ Philip III

5. ___ Olivares

6. ___ Henry of Navarre

7. ___ Wallenstein

8. ___ Gustavus Adolphus

9. ___ Battle of Nordlingen—1635

10. ___ Battle of Rocroi—1643

11. ___ Louis XIV

12. ___ Prince Eugene of Savoy

13. ___ Kara Mustapha

A) left government of Spain to Duke of Lerma
B) scourge of humanity
C) Catholic commander of Hapsburg army
D) King of Sweden; Lion of the North
E) Prince Ferdinand won against the Swedes

F) defeated Turks in the Battle of Zenta
G) warned Galileo on behalf of Pope Paul V
H) wrote the *Principia Mathematica*
I) "Sun King"; Motto—I am the State
J) Englishman–discovered circulation of blood

K) French defeated Spanish in Thirty Years War
L) King of France; founded Bourbon dynasty
M) Philip IV's chief minister; upright man

Mini-Essay Question: State the effects of the Treaty of Westphalia regarding
(Extra credit—4 points.) Christendom and nationalism.

Personal Opinion: Name an important or interesting fact that you learned in this chapter. How could this fact affect your life?

Supplemental Reading

F. A. Forbes. *St. Vincent de Paul*. TAN.

Autobiography of St. Margaret Mary Alacoque. TAN.

Mary Fabyan Windeatt. *St. Margaret Mary*. TAN.

Perfect Score: 100
(Each Question is worth 2 points.)

Score: _____

Completion

Directions: Complete and make each statement true and accurate by writing one or more words on each blank line.

1. Many historians believe that the _____ , which turned James I against Catholics, was organized by Robert Cecil.

2. The Act of Uniformity resulted in the Separatists leaving England and coming to America in 1620. They were later known as the _____ . The _____ were English Calvinists who wanted to make the church of England more like Calvinist churches.

3. Charles I was a _____ Church Anglican who insisted on the full Anglican rituals (candles, incense, etc).

4. The Royalist/Covenanter force at _____ was defeated by Cromwell.

5. Cromwell's rule between the reign of King Charles I and Charles II is known as the Puritan or Cromwellian _____ .

6. The _____ which was passed by Parliament required office holders to take public communion in the Anglican Church.

7. James II had first been married to a Catholic by the name of _____ , who died of cancer.

8. Upon the birth of his heir, James Francis Edward Stuart, James II was betrayed by his two daughters _____ and _____ , and their husbands, William and George.

9. The _____ Laws, severely restricted the life of Irish Catholics in all areas, in an attempt to do away with them.

10. The persecuted Irish attended Mass in secret places called _____ and sent their children to hidden schools called _____ .

11. Supporters of James II's son James, who was a Catholic in exile in France, are known as _____ .

12. James married Clementina Sobieski and had two sons, _____ and _____ (who became a Cardinal).

13. King George's son William, the Duke of _____ , fought attempts by Bonnie Prince Charlie to regain the throne.

14. With the end of the Stuart Dynasty, _____ and _____ triumphed in England.

Multiple Choice

Directions: After each statement below, there is a set of words or phrases. Circle the letter next to the one word or phrase that best completes the sentence.

1. Which of the following resulted from of the *Glorious Revolution*?
    a) Parliment became dominant in England.
    b) Protestantism triumphed over Catholicism.
    c) England became a world leader.
    d) a. and b only
    e) a. and c only

2. Cecil claimed that the following was a plot of Catholics to blow up Parliament and James I and his two sons:
    a) the Clarendon Plot
    b) the Restoration Plot
    c) the Titus Oates Plot
    d) the Gunpowder Plot

3. James I did all of the following except
    a) increased laws against Catholics
    b) enforced the Act of Uniformity
    c) permitted Parliament to pass the Clarendon Code
    d) broke the treaty with Ireland

4. The rejection of the Church of England by the Scottish Calvinists resulted in the meeting in Edinburgh at Greyfriars Church where they signed the
   a) Allegiance of Edinburgh
   b) Act of Succession
   c) Covenant
   d) none of the above

5. The measure passed by Parliament and John Pym on November 23, 1640 to condemn King Charles I's policies (shortly before they attempted to impeach the Queen) was called the
   a) Grand Remonstrance
   b) Grand Impeachment
   c) Grand Condemnation
   d) Grand Revolution

6. The First Civil War in England between the Royalists (or Cavaliers) and the Roundheads (the Puritans) ended with a Roundhead victory (including the capturing of 5,000 prisoners and placing of King Charles under house arrest) at the
   a) Battle of Naseby
   b) Battle of Limerick
   c) Battle of Culloden
   d) none of the above

7. The fleeing of Irishmen who were given the choice of death or exile after the English under Cromwell forced them into the province of Connaught is known as the
   a) "Flight of the Weary Ones"
   b) "Flight of the Wild Geese"
   c) "Flight of the Soldier Boys"
   d) "Flight of the Night Soldiers"

8. Upon assuming the throne of England, James II
   a) annulled all anti-Catholic laws (including the Test Act)
   b) published a Declaration of Indulgence (all are equal under the law)
   c) allowed Mass to be celebrated in public
   d) a. and b. only
   e) all of the above

9. By signing the treaty of Limerick, William of Orange and Sarsfield ended the
   a) War of English Succession
   b) War of Limerick
   c) The Second Civil War
   d) none of the above

10. The attempt to assume the throne by Bonnie Prince Charlie in 1745, which began with his landing in Scotland with seven companions, was called
    a) "The '25"
    b) "The '35"
    c) "The '45"
    d) "The '55"

True/False

Directions: Circle the letter T if the statement is true or F if the statement is false.

1. T F James I believed in the *Divine Right of Kings*, as did Charles V and Philip II.

2. T F Parliament was dissolved by Charles I, Charles II and Oliver Cromwell.

3. T F The Covenanters won easily over Charles' army, and he felt forced to sign the Pacification of Berwick, which ended the First Scots War.

4. T F The Short Parliament refers to the dissolving of Parliament in less than a month because the Puritans won the elections to most of the seats in the House of Commons.

5. T F The Rump Parliament occurred during the time of the Short Parliament.

6. T F Although Cromwell enforced Puritan standards, he still allowed Christmas to be celebrated in England.

7. T F It is estimated that half of the native population of Ireland perished under Cromwell's rule.

8. T F Although Richard Cromwell tried to succeed his father as Lord Protector, people wanted Charles II because they were tired of Puritanism.

9. T F Charles II, despite his many concessions to Parliament, in the end remained loyal to his wife and brother.

10. T F William of Orange's triumphant march into London to assume the throne after betraying James II is called the Great Revolution.

11. T F The War of English Succession was an attempt to free Scotland from English rule.

12. T F The treaty signed by William of Orange and Sarsfield severely limited the rights of the Irish people.

13. T   F   The Treaty Stone can be seen even today in the Limerick city square. It is a constant reminder of the deceit practiced on the Irish after the Treaty of Limerick.

Matching

Directions: This list is made up of names of persons, groups, places and things. Each one corresponds to one of the lettered phrases below. In each blank, write the letter of the phrase that correctly identifies that person, group, place or thing.

1. ___ Guy Fawkes

2. ___ Act of Uniformity

3. ___ Henrietta Maria

4. ___ Oliver Cromwell

5. ___ Puritans

6. ___ Father Huddleston

7. ___ Restoration

8. ___ Catherine of Braganza

9. ___ Clarendon Code

10. ___ Mary of Modena

11. ___ William of Orange

12. ___ Bishop Oliver Plunkett

13. ___ Patrick Sarsfield

A) assisted Charles II in death

B) French Catholic Princess; wife of Charles I

C) Italian Catholic Princess; wife of James II

D) Lord Protector of England

E) provided penalties for non-Anglicans

F) great Irish General; fought William

G) betrayed James II; he and Mary were crowned

H) martyred in Titus Oates Plot; now a saint

I) Portuguese Catholic princess; wife of Charles II

J) required all to attend Anglican services

K) Roundheads; lost to Royalists at Edgehill

L) return of Stuarts to throne of England

M) stood guard over barrels of gunpowder

Mini-Essay Question:
(Extra credit—4 points.)
List two important and lasting results of the Glorious Revolution.

Personal Opinion:
Name an important or interesting fact that you learned in this chapter. How could this fact affect your life?

Supplemental Reading

Fr. Alban Butler. *Lives of the Saints*. TAN. (Article on Oliver Plunkett, Bishop and Martyr.)

CHRIST THE KING, LORD OF HISTORY — WORKBOOK

Perfect Score: 100
(Each Question is worth 2 points.)

Score: _____

Completion

Directions: Complete and make each statement true and accurate by writing one or more words on each blank line.

1. The _____formed a partially secret organization in Paris, France in the 18th century that aimed at substituting itself for the Church.

2. Jean Jacques _____ held that every man's mind is pure and should be protected from the corrupting influences of any authority—Church, king, parents.

3. Voltaire wanted to eliminate all _____ , which tries to tell men what to do and which he considered evil.

4. _____ is the philosophy which rejects moral absolutes and authority, especially religious authority.

5. Although Louis XIV's grandson did become King of Spain, the French guaranteed that its government and that of Spain would never be _____ .

6. Charles III did everything in his power to suppress the Church, including expelling the _____ from Spain and threatening to take Spain into schism if Pope Clement XIV did not disband that order.

7. In England, the _____ movement took the lands away from peasant farmers, forcing them to become tenants or unemployed.

8. In England, two Catholic _____ Bills removed penalties which had been imposed on Catholics by Protestants earlier.

9. The key battle in the Seven Years War was the Battle of Quebec, Canada, also known as the _____ War.

10. Catherine the Great was the person who was most responsible for _____ being partitioned and she seized the Crimea and the Caucasus from Turkey.

11. The _____ is the document through which Charles VI tried to get Maria Teresa recognized throughout Europe as the rightful ruler of Austria.

12. After Hungary helped her to win the war, Maria Teresa worked in freeing the peasants, training and equipping the _____ , and then reforming taxes and setting up a new, fairer system of _____ .

13. The patriotic rebellion of 1768 in Poland was led by Bishop _____ and Casimir _____ .

14. The partition of Poland occurred because Catherine the Great decided not to rule the country through Polish kings but to annex Poland to _____ .

Multiple Choice

Directions: After each statement below, there is a set of words or phrases. Circle the letter next to the one word or phrase that best completes the sentence.

1. Europe's moral decline and rejection of authority—especially in France, which dominated Europe not only politically, but culturally and intellectually—reached bottom in the
   a) 16th Century
   b) 17th Century
   c) 18th Century
   d) 19th Century

2. The uniting of Europe behind the Holy Roman Emperor, Leopold I, to prevent the uniting of France and Spain under one ruler is called the
   a) War Against France
   b) War of the French Succession
   c) War Against Spain
   d) War of the Spanish Succession

3. The key battle of the Holy Roman Empire against France was
   a) the Battle of Blenheim
   b) the Battle of Paris
   c) the Battle of Rome
   d) none of the above

4. After the Society of Jesus was suppressed, it did not become re-established until
   a) 1814
   b) 1874
   c) 1914
   d) 1974

5. Because of the rivalry for trade in the New World, the wars between France and England were fought both in Europe and the New World. Their most significant war was the
   a) Seven Country War
   b) Seven Years War
   c) Seven Days War
   d) Seventeen Years War

6. When the Americans needed assistance in their War for Independence, aid was provided by the:
   a) Spanish
   b) Germans
   c) English
   d) French

7. The European leaders who believed in absolute power while adopting many liberal ideas, especially contempt for religion, are known as
   a) the Despot Rulers
   b) Enlightened Despots
   c) Enlightened Anarchists
   d) none of the above

8. The War of the Austrian Succession which was concluded in 1748 resulted in which of the following:
   a) Maria Teresa's husband, Francis Stephen, was elected Holy Roman Emperor
   b) Austria was recognized throughout Europe as a major power
   c) the Holy Roman Empire had become strong again
   d) a. and c. only
   e) all of the above

9. The main concerns of Maria Teresa during her reign included all of the following except
   a) making Austria a strong nation
   b) improving the lives of Austrian citizens
   c) insuring the security of the succession of her throne
   d) raising her 16 children

10. Typical of 18th-century European rule (except for that of Maria Teresa) were all of the following except
    a) warfare
    b) absolutism
    c) liberalism
    d) irreligion
    e) limited government

True/False

Directions: Circle the letter T if the statement is true or F if the statement is false.

1. T F The Nine Brothers was the most important Freemasonic lodge in Paris, with members such as Voltaire, Danton and others participating.

2. T F Voltaire's liberal argument was that men must be free to speak and print anything they wish and to live by any moral standard they choose—even if they have none.

3. T F Liberalism usually approves of the elimination of opposition, but never by violence.

4. T F Charles III, Philip V's son, ruled Spain as an absolutist very similar to Richelieu of France.

5. T F Louis XV was an able ruler.

6. T F The Bourbons expelled the Dominicans because that Order was a spiritually powerful force which opposed their agenda.

7. T F 18th-century England was a country which preferred the use of long prison terms to capital punishment for crimes.

8. T F The French and Indian War resulted in France being the dominant power in the New World.

9. T F Prior to the 18th century, Russia did not have a significant impact on the history of the world.

10. T F Because he helped Russia become a power in Europe, the Russian Senate gave Peter the title of "The Great."

11. T F Catherine is known as "The Great" because of her concern for the people and her just punishments.

12. T F Frederick the Great of Prussia founded the Academy of Science and Literature to spread liberal ideas.

13. T F The one serious blot on Maria Teresa's record as a great ruler is the part she played in the partition of Germany.

Matching

Directions: This list is made up of names of persons, groups, places and things. Each one corresponds to one of the lettered phrases below. In each blank, write the letter of the phrase that correctly identifies that person, group, place or thing.

1. ___ a lodge

2. ___ Rousseau

3. ___ Mesmer

4. ___ Age of Reason

5. ___ Charles II

6. ___ Tsar (Czar)

7. ___ Paul, son of Catherine

8. ___ Prussia

9. ___ Frederick the Great

10. ___ Poland

11. ___ King Augustus II

12. ___ Stanislaus Augustus

13. ___ 1795

A) wrote the *Social Contract*
B) founded Academy of Science and Literature
C) Russian word for emperor
D) a group of Freemasons
E) Protestant state in northeast Germany
F) passed law prohibiting women rulers in Russia
G) ruined economically by fighting Swedes and Turks
H) last Spanish Hapsburg
I) Poland destroyed by Russia, Prussia and Austria
J) The Enlightenment
K) was elected Polish King by Russian manipulation
L) crushed a patriotic rebellion in 1768
M) liberal scientist— performed rites, cast spells

Mini-Essay Question: Explain why the eighteenth century is known as the Age of
(Extra credit—4 points.) Reason or the Enlightenment.

Personal Opinion: Name an important or interesting fact that you learned in this chapter. How could this fact affect your life?

Supplemental Reading

Brother Charles Madden. *Freemasonry—Mankind's Hidden Enemy*. TAN.

Perfect Score: 100
(Each Question is worth 2 points.)

Score: _____

Completion

Directions: Complete and make each statement true and accurate by writing one or more words on each blank line.

1. The French Revolution is a pivotal event in the history of Western civilization because of the enemies the Church has had to fight ever since and the

   consequences in our own time, such as _____ .

2. The two forces which worked against Louis and Antoinette to convince the people

   that they were really bad were the wealthy _____ of France,

   who wrote vicious pamphlets about them, and the _____ , who
   hated their authority and so spread lies through immoral writings.

3. Before Louis actually had the Estates General meet, he asked the people for Lists

   of _____ .

4. When the Third Estate, dominated by liberal lawyers, broke away from the others,

   it became known as the _____ and identified itself as the
   official legislating body of France.

5. The Storming of the _____ on July 14, 1789, in which the
   violent mob killed the guards in an old prison, freeing only seven prisoners, became
   a symbol of freedom. (July 14 is still celebrated as France's Independence Day).

6. The difference between the Catholic political tradition and the French
   Revolutionary Liberalism is that Catholicism states that rights come from

   _____ , and therefore may be taken away by no one, whereas

   Liberalism sees rights as coming from the state or the _____ ,
   so they may be taken away by those entities.

7. In October 1789 the _____ , a group which preached that man should have complete freedom to do whatever he wanted, emerged and remained powerful throughout the Revolution.

8. The failure of the French royal family's Flight to _____ was due to: traveling in a berline, procrastination, the panic of Leonard and dispersing of troops from Ste. Menehould and an innkeeper's betrayal.

9. Less than half of the priests took the oath to the Civil Constitution of the Clergy.

   Those who did not were called _____ priests, and they ministered to the people in secret.

10. Twenty-three years of war for France and Europe began when the legislative assembly declared war on _____ as a means to unite the country.

11. Led by the Marquis de Rochejacquelein and Cathelineau, the Rising in the _____ was an attempt by the priests, nobles and peasants in the Catholic farming region in western France to show their opposition to the Revolution after the King was killed.

12. The revolutionists were so anti-God that they made a whole new calendar just to abolish _____ , forbidding the worship of God in favor of the goddess of _____ and setting up a communist economy.

13. With his new _____ Republic in place in July 1797, and with the conquest of Holland, Switzerland and Italy by May 1798, Napoleon was almost unstoppable. He even determined that when Pope Pius VI died, the army would prevent another election.

14. In the Italian uprising against the French in May 1799, the people uprooted the "Trees of Liberty," replacing them with _____ , while the _____ overthrew revolutionary regimes in Naples, Rome and Florence.

Multiple Choice

Directions: After each statement below, there is a set of words or phrases. Circle the letter next to the one word or phrase that best completes the sentence.

1. The Catholic kingdom of Louis IX and the High Middle Ages were destroyed by which of the following?
   - a) the Protestant Revolt
   - b) the Wars of Religion
   - c) the absolutism created by Richelieu
   - d) the extravagance and corruptions of Kings Louis XIV and XV
   - e) a. and c. only
   - f) all of the above

2. Although Louis XVI inherited a terrible situation in France, he began to make changes immediately which included all of the following except
   - a) he began the custom of *corvee*, which helped peasants
   - b) he ordered that no taxes be increased
   - c) he reduced expenditures at Versailles
   - d) he improved conditions in prisons, abolishing the torture of accused prisoners
   - e) he re-established local parliaments

3. The Estates General consisted of all except
   - a) noblemen
   - b) royalty
   - c) clergy
   - d) ordinary citizens

4. The Lists of Grievances Louis XVI received from the people showed that they wanted which of the following?
   - a) a fair tax
   - b) retention of the Catholic monarchy
   - c) an end to the Catholic monarchy
   - d) a. and b. only
   - e) a. and c. only

5. From July 12-14 ,1789, at the beginning of the Revolution, when the mobs ran wild in the streets and burned police headquarters, conditions in Paris included:
   - a) high unemployment
   - b) hunger and wheat shortages
   - c) agitation of the crowd by the liberals
   - d) a. and c. only
   - e) all of the above

6. In August 1789, the violence and anarchy experienced throughout the French countryside was known as the
        a) Great Fear
        b) Dark Night
        c) August Massacre
        d) Destruction of the Emigres

7. The Revolution's murdering of 1400 prisoners (men, women and children) along with all non-juring priests (who are now considered martyrs by the Church), is called the
        a) Avenging Massacres
        b) September Massacres
        c) Destruction of the Emigres
        d) none of the above

8. The execution of King Louis XVI was the beginning of the:
        a) September Massacres
        b) Coup d'Etat of Brumaire
        c) Reign of Terror
        d) Thermidorian Reaction

9. The overthrow of Robespierre by the convention leaders under Joseph Fouche (co-governor of Lyon) was known as the
        a) September Massacres
        b) Coup d'Etat of Brumaire
        c) Reign of Terror
        d) Thermidorian Reaction

10. On November 9, 1799, Napoleon became First Consul after he and his troops overcame the Council of Five Hundred (France's newest legislative body). This is known as the
        a) September Massacres
        b) Coup d'Etat of Brumaire
        c) Reign of Terror
        d) Thermidorian Reaction

True/False

Directions: Circle the letter T if the statement is true or F if the statement is false.

1.   T   F   Marie Antoinette said "Let them eat cake," referring to the hungry poor who had no bread.

2.   T   F   Louis and Antoinette were victims of the evils which had begun long before them.

3.   T   F   Louis and Antoinette were very popular with the ordinary people for the first ten years of their reign.

4.　T　F　The Liberals were able to dominate the Estates General because it did not meet as was customary, but instead met as a mass, with each person's vote counting individually.

5.　T　F　The Tennis Court Oath was taken by the Noblemen of the First Estate to procure a new government and constitution for France.

6.　T　F　The terminology of left and right, which is used today in the United States, comes from the French Revolution, where conservatives sat on the right of the assembly and liberals on the left.

7.　T　F　The Civil Constitution of the Clergy, along with the seizing of Church land and suppressing of orders and vows, were attempts by the Assembly to get rid of the Church in France.

8.　T　F　The Swiss Guard and everyone in the palace of the Tuileries (800 people in all) were massacred by the angry mob which marched from Marseilles to Paris.

9.　T　F　The Duke of Carra's greed for the Blue Diamond of the Golden Fleece is the reason for the throwing of the Battle of Valmy, discarding a last good chance to overthrow the Revolution and save the royal family.

10.　T　F　Following the abolition of the French monarchy on September 21, 1792, Louis was found guilty; on January 21, 1793 he was executed by a firing squad and his family imprisoned.

11.　T　F　The Law of 22 Prairial allowed for limited defense for those persons sentenced to die by the Revolutionary Tribunal.

12.　T　F　The Carmelite nuns of Compiegne just escaped death, thanks to the efforts of Joseph Fouche and the Convention, who stopped the Terror.

13.　T　F　Shortly after the ratification of the Constitution of the Year VIII had established Napoleon as dictator of France, the cardinals in conclave elected as pope a former monk, Pope Pius VII, thus beginning a fifteen-year struggle between the two.

Matching

Directions: This list is made up of names of persons, groups, places and things. Each one corresponds to one of the lettered phrases below. In each blank, write the letter of the phrase that correctly identifies that person, group, place or thing.

1. ___ Mirabeau

2. ___ Talleyrand

3. ___ Axel Ferson

4. ___ Drouet

5. ___ Barnave

6. ___ Robespierre

7. ___ Danton

8. ___ Marat

9. ___ Charlotte Corday

10. ___ Napoleon

11. ___ Horatio Nelson

12. ___ Cardinal Ruffo

13. ___ Cardinal Chiaramonti

A) Jacobin leader of the Paris Commune

B) violent, militant atheist with diseased body

C) commander of the Assembly's Army of the Alps

D) author of the Civil Constitution; liberal Bishop

E) made Congregation of the Holy Faith/ Sanfedisti

F) assassinated Marat hoping to save France

G) angry innkeeper— thwarted the Flight to Varennes

H) Swedish—planned the Flight to Varennes

I) Assemblies Guard—later helped the royal family

J) Pope Pius VII; challenged Napoleon for 15 years

K) Liberal leader of the National Assembly

L) British Admiral who beat Napoleon in Egypt

M) established Revolutionary Tribunal; converted, tried to end Terror

Mini-Essay Question:
(Extra credit—4 points.)

State the liberals' attitude and the Jacobins' attitude and tell whether these two positions were or were not in harmony.

Personal Opinion:

Name an important or interesting fact that you learned in this chapter. How could this fact affect your life?

Supplemental Reading

Professor Robin Anderson. *Pope Pius VII: His Life, Times and Struggle with Napoleon in the Aftermath of the French Revolution.* TAN.

25	THE AGE OF NAPOLEON	Text Pages 346-368

Perfect Score: 100
(Each Question is worth 2 points.)

Score: _____

Completion

Directions: Complete and make each statement true and accurate by writing one or more words on each blank line.

1. Napoleon's foreign minister was _____ , while the Minister of

   Police was Joseph _____ .

2. Napoleon's goal of building a colonial Empire, with the _____
   territory as his base and Sant Domingue as a shipping base was dissolved when
   he failed to regain Haiti and ended up selling the territory to the new U.S.
   Government.

3. When Napoleon tried to overcome Switzerland in 1803, he broke the Treaty of

   _____ , which had been made with England in March of 1802,
   so England declared war.

4. Although Admiral Horatio Nelson died, the British fleet defeated Napoleon at

   Cape _____ , playing a crucial role in his ultimate defeat.

5. Although Napoleon won the battles at _____ and

   _____ and was able to incorporate Prussia into the French
   Empire, he incurred the wrath of General Blucher, which was to cost him dearly.

6. Napoleon annexed the Papal States, despite the refusal of Pope

   _____ to go along with the proposal. When Napoleon
   imprisoned the Pope, it appeared as though the sword had triumphed over the
   spirit.

7. Palafox first went to the chapel of the _____ to ask her
   intercession and then turned his city into a military state.

8. Although the Zaragozans finally lost their battle on February 21, 1809, they
   inspired other Spaniards to continue fighting the French with

   _____ warfare.

CHAPTER 25 — THE AGE OF NAPOLEON   145

9. Hofer and the other peasants did not want the _____ area of Austria to be given to Bavaria, so they fought three battles on Berg Isel, the mountain overlooking the city of Innsbruck. Even though Hofer was finally caught and executed on February 20, 1810, he is still thought of as a hero.

10. During Napoleon's six months in _____ , he lost all but 1000 troops and some stragglers. His Grand Army was destroyed.

11. The allied leaders who formed a five-man provisional government with Talleyrand as the head met at the Congress of _____ , which was transformed from a peace conference into a council of war after Napoleon returned to France.

12. After the troops turned on Marshall Ney and joined Napoleon, they allowed him to come back into Paris and begin ruling France again. This was known as the rule of the _____ .

13. Prince Clemens Metternich, Prime Minister of the Hapsburg Empire, was the traditionalist leader of Europe after The Holy Roman Empire dissolved under Napoleon. He developed _____ Diplomacy, worked to maintain the balance of power between the nations and assisted in the adoption of the _____ Decrees, which offered oversight to printed materials taught in Austrian universities to prevent the spread of revolutionary ideas.

14. The suffering which Spain endured in the 20th century as a result of liberalism might have been avoided had the rightful kings, the _____ , succeeded in coming to power.

Multiple Choice

Directions: After each statement below, there is a set of words or phrases. Circle the letter next to the one word or phrase that best completes the sentence.

1. Napoleon wanted to conquer which of the following
   a) all of Europe
   b) Asia
   c) America
   d) all of the above

2. The key battle Napoleon waged with Italy was the
        a) Battle of Ulm
        b) Battle of the Nations
        c) Battle of Marengo
        d) none of the above

3. The Battle of Three Emperors at which Alexander I, Francis II and Napoleon were all present occurred at
        a) Vienna
        b) Austerlitz
        c) Jena
        d) Berlin

4. Napoleon's goals in centralizing the educational system under the University of France included all of the following except
        a) to weaken tradition
        b) to weaken the Church's influence
        c) to make France a leader in education in Europe
        d) to indoctrinate children with revolutionary ideas

5. The resistance of the Spaniards to the French, after French troops had killed hundreds of Spaniards on May 2, 1808, was known as the
        a) Continental Blockade
        b) Peninsular War
        c) French and Spanish War
        d) Hundred Days War

6. For the four years that Napoleon insisted upon fighting the Spaniards, he lost a daily average of
        a) 10 men
        b) 50 men
        c) 75 men
        d) 100 men

7. The two countries whose Catholic peasants rebelled against Napoleon were
        a) Spain and Austria
        b) Spain and Portugal
        c) Austria and Portugal
        d) Austria and Belgium

8. The Allied troops of Austria, Russia and Prussia, in October of 1813, won the battle that ultimately gave them the capture of Paris in March of 1814, forcing Napoleon to abdicate. This battle is known as the
        a) Battle of Ulm
        b) Battle of Vitoria
        c) Battle of the Nations
        d) Battle of Waterloo

9. The third and most crucial mistake Napoleon made on Waterloo day was:
   a) not sending reinforcements to General Ney and delaying attack for half an hour
   b) tying up two divisions that he would need later, one at the Vendee rising and the other at the Chateau
   c) overconfidence in his ability to win the battle and contempt for Wellington, because of which he delayed the beginning of the battle
   d) none of the above

10. The defeat of Napoleon at Waterloo was due to which of the following:
   a) Wellington's brilliance and strategy as a commander and the heroism of his British soldiers.
   b) General Blucher and his Prussian soldiers who could not be stopped
   c) the Vendee Rising
   d) the mistakes Napoleon made
   e) all of the above

True/False

Directions: Circle the letter T if the statement is true or F if the statement is false.

1. T F In order to avoid schism, Pope Pius VII made concessions to Napoleon, while Napoleon, for his part, conceded to the Church those things he felt would be to his advantage in the future. Both were subject to anger from people who thought they should not have made concessions.

2. T F Napoleon sent Tallyrand to negotiate with the Pope for the sake of appearances so that the French people (who were loyal Catholics) would continue to support him.

3. T F When Napoleon founded the University of France, this was only the second time in the history of any country where there was such centralized control over the educational system.

4. T F The Continental Blockade referred to the suppression of trade between countries under Napoleon's dominion and the country of Russia.

5. T F The Zaragozans would not submit to Joseph Bonaparte as King of Spain because they despised Napoleon and everything he stood for (his hatred of the Church and his embodiment of the evil French Revolution).

6. T F From June 15 to August 13, 1808 the French lost so many soldiers that the French General decided to pull out of Zaragoza.

7. T F The French commander, General Soult, devised the Lines of Torres Vedres strategy against British troops.

8.   T   F   As a result of the Battle of Vitoria, in which the English won the victory over the French, Spain now belonged to England.

9.   T   F   The political leaders in Europe after Napoleon's fall were divided into two groups: the revolutionaries and the counter-revolutionaries (traditionalists).

10.   T   F   In light of the Salic Law, Isabel (daughter of Ferdinand VII and Maria Christina) should never have come to the throne of Spain, the rightful king being Carlos V.

11.   T   F   During the Second Carlist War, General Tomas Zumalacarregui was killed in the battle at Bilbao because Carlos did not listen to his advice to continue on.

12.   T   F   After twenty years under Isabel, even her government could not stand her immoral, scandalous lifestyle and so deposed her, choosing King Amadeo I (an Italian) to be ruler of Spain.

13.   T   F   After the collapse of the First Spanish Republic, Alfonso took the throne, the Carlist movement collapsed, Charles VII left Spain and the liberals were left in control.

Matching

Directions: This list is made up of names of persons, groups, places and things. Each one corresponds to one of the lettered phrases below. In each blank, write the letter of the phrase that correctly identifies that person, group, place or thing.

1. ___ Concordat

2. ___ Organic Articles

3. ___ Villeneuve

4. ___ General Radet

5. ___ Zaragoza, Spain

6. ___ Jose Palafox

7. ___ Augustina Zaragoza

8. ___ Andreas Hofer

9. ___ Sir Arthur Wellesley

10. ___ Mikhail Kutusov

11. ___ The Cortes

12. ___ Alfonso

13. ___ Carlist Movement

A) Viscount Wellington of Talavera

B) capital of Aragon; city of Our Lady of the Pillar

C) Spain's traditional law-making body

D) a code of ecclesiastical law; restricted the Church

E) agreement between a government and the Vatican

F) Liberal ruler of Spain; son of Isabel

G) leader of the junta of Zaragoza

H) seized cannon; stopped French from entering Zaragoza

I) supported Carlos V (Spanish traditionalist) as King

J) Admiral of Combined Fleet; wouldn't attack Nelson

K) leader of the Austrian peasant rebellion

L) Russian General who defended Moscow

M) arrested Pope Pius VII on July 5, 1809

Mini-Essay Question:
(Extra credit—4 points.)

Describe the philosophy and political ideas of Prince Metternich (Counter-Revolutionary leader).

Personal Opinion:

Name an important or interesting fact that you learned in this chapter. How could this fact affect your life?

Perfect Score: 100
(Each Question is worth 2 points.)

Score: _____

Completion

Directions: Complete and make each statement true and accurate by writing one or more words on each blank line.

1. In the economic system of the Middle Ages called _____ , each individual had access to the means of production. A person owned his own tools, equipment and land and he could be self-supporting; therefore, the wealth was more evenly distributed.

2. The primary elements of Marxist Communism were socialism, atheism and the

   _____ , a philosophy declaring that all reality is explained by violent struggle. This was used to justify violence in overthrowing Capitalism.

3. The ideas that religion had been invented by those in power to oppress the weak and that the workers of the world were to unite were expressed in the Communist

   _____ .

4. Among the many reforms made by Franz Josef, the taxation system, judiciary system and educational system were all reformed, careers in the Imperial service

   were opened to men of every class, and the " _____ " was abolished (the requirement that peasants had to do a certain amount of work for landlords).

5. The Austrian Empire under Franz Josef had industrialization without the evils

   of laissez-faire _____ .

6. To unite Italy under his rule, Count Camillo Cavour (Prime Minister of

   Piedmont-Sardinia) wanted to get _____ out of Lombardy and Venetia.

7. From the Battle of _____ , when the Austrians lost to the Prussians, until World War I (for 48 years), Franz Josef kept Austria at peace.

8. Franz Josef made concessions to the liberals by setting up the _____ in which there were parliaments in both Austria and Hungary that would be mostly independent of each other, with Franz over both.

9. In the new German Empire, Bismark put into effect an anti-Catholic policy called the _____ (culture war).

10. The Count de Chambord asked that the traditional flag of France be restored in order for him to be king of France. The assembly voted; the liberals won by one vote and set up the Third _____ .

11. When Garibaldi annexed Rome and made it the capital of the Kingdom of Italy, the Pope (with no territory now) became known as the _____ of the Vatican.

12. _____ is the drive of European nations for political and economic control over other, non-Western areas, such as Asia, Africa or the Middle East.

13. The population of Ireland was severely affected by the potato famine in the 1840's. The Irish died of hunger, epidemics and the conditions on board the " _____ " ships, on which almost as many people arrived in America dead as alive.

14. The Rising of '98 and the Easter _____ were efforts by the Irish to gain independence from Great Britain.

Multiple Choice

Directions: After each statement below, there is a set of words or phrases. Circle the letter next to the one word or phrase that best completes the sentence.

1. The economic system whereby wealth, power and the means of production are concentrated in the hands of a few is called
   - a) capitalism
   - b) distributism
   - c) socialism
   - d) communism

2. The economic system whereby the means of production are owned and controlled by the government is called
   a) capitalism
   b) distributism
   c) socialism
   d) communism

3. The type of Socialists that believed that property should be redistributed by force were called
   a) Utopians
   b) Fabians
   c) Communists
   d) Capitalists

4. Russia's conflict with Turkey which began on October 1, 1853, and in which England and France entered on Turkey's side, is known as
   a) the Seven Weeks War
   b) the Battle of Solferino
   c) the Crimean War
   d) none of the above

5. Franz Josef's Austrian army faced Napoleon III's army (which was assisting Count Cavour and the Italians in the fighting) in:
   a) the Seven Weeks War
   b) the Battle at Solferino
   c) the Crimean War
   d) none of the above

6. In June of 1866, Austria began fighting Prussia in:
   a) the Seven Weeks War
   b) the Battle of Solferino
   c) the Crimean War
   d) none of the above

7. In 1871, the Paris Commune took over Paris by overthrowing Napoleon III; it established the Committee of Public Safety and killed many people. The Versailles army finally overcame the Committee and vengefully killed many others in
   a) Semaine Sanglante
   b) Bloody Sunday
   c) the Commune War
   d) none of the above

8. Pope Pius IX is responsible for
   a) proclaiming the doctrine of the Immaculate Conception
   b) the encyclical *Rerum Novarum*
   c) issuing the *Syllabus of Errors* condemning Liberalism
   d) a. and c. only
   e) all of the above

9. Great Britain as the first Imperialist power is an example of imperialism at its best and worst. The assistance of imperialist England was to the advantage of which country:

> a) India
> b) China
> c) Africa
> d) none of the above

10. Following the British reign of terror, Ireland was given the choice of another war, or independence for 26 counties with the counties of Ulster remaining part of Great Britain. These other counties numbered:

> a) four counties
> b) five counties
> c) six counties
> d) seven counties

True/False

Directions: Circle the letter T if the statement is true or F if the statement is false.

1. T F Laissez-faire refers to the intervention of government in the affairs of capitalists and requires them to treat their employees fairly.

2. T F The Factory Act was enacted in 1833 to protect men from poor working conditions.

3. T F Marx and Engels believed the proletariat should unite and overthrow the social order, setting up a communist society by force.

4. T F The revolution which began on July 17, 1830 in France was the result of hostility toward King Louis XVIII.

5. T F Like Metternich, Franz Josef, who assumed the throne on December 2, 1848, was totally dedicated to God and his people.

6. T F As a result of the battle at Solferino, Austria lost major territory when Franz Josef gave up Lombardy and Venetia.

7. T F Franz Josef looked forward to the marriage of Franz Ferdinand to Sophie Chotek because he hoped one of their children would become heir to the throne.

8. T F Because of his social encyclicals in which he advocated correcting the evils of the Industrial Revolution by respecting workers and giving them fair hours and wages, etc., Leo XIII is recognized as one of the greatest men of the nineteenth century.

9. T F English imperialism in China resulted in the building of a profitable opium trade for England and in the British smashing of the Taiping Rebellion, thereby protecting the British opium trade.

10. T F The European imperialist movement into Africa was good because it brought Christianity, but bad because when the Africans attempted to gain independence, liberalism and Communism became strong forces in Africa.

11. T F In 1829, when the Irish petitioned for emancipation (rights of citizenship), the British Parliament was angry and retaliated.

12. T F When Padraic Pearse and the other Irish leaders surrendered (in order to protect the people) at the end of the Easter Rebellion, all the leaders except one were executed.

13. T F In the partition of Ireland, independence was granted to 26 counties, with the remaining six staying under Great Britain.

Matching

Directions: This list is made up of names of persons, groups, places and things. Each one corresponds to one of the lettered phrases below. In each blank, write the letter of the phrase that correctly identifies that person, group, place or thing.

1. ___ James Watt

2. ___ Hegel

3. ___ Catherine Labouré

4. ___ Louis Philippe

5. ___ Louis Napoleon

6. ___ Padraic Pearse

7. ___ Sisi

8. ___ Bismarck

9. ___ Raoul Rigault

10. ___ Sophie Chotek

11. ___ Quirinal Palace

12. ___ White Fathers

13. ___ Wolfe Tone

A) German—taught the philosophy of the dialectic
B) ruler whose goal was to unite German states under Prussia
C) Protestant founder of the United Irish Movement
D) morganatic marriage to Franz Ferdinand
E) married Spanish countess Eugenie Montijo
F) Elizabeth—Franz Josef's wife from Bavaria
G) leader—Committee of Public Safety
H) French missionary priests to Africa
I) replaced Charles X; known as "Citizen King"
J) led Easter Rebellion
K) had visions—Our Lady of the Miraculous Medal
L) residence of the Pope
M) invented steam engine—began Industrial Revolution

Mini-Essay Question: How did the Industrial Revolution affect people's economic
(Extra credit—4 points.) independence?

Personal Opinion: Name an important or interesting fact that you learned in this chapter. How could this fact affect your life?

Supplemental Reading

Fr. Joseph Dirvin, C.M. *St. Catherine Labouré of the Miraculous Medal*. TAN.

Mary Alice Dennis. *Melanie—And the Story of Our Lady of La Salette*. TAN.

Perfect Score: 100
(Each Question is worth 2 points.)

Score: _____

Completion

Directions: Complete and make each statement true and accurate by writing one or more words on each blank line.

1. The traditionalist movement in France was badly hurt in 1894 by the

   _____ Case.

2. Essen, Germany was home to the _____ Arms Works, which was the largest business in Europe.

3. From 1894 to 1914, the assassination of six heads of state of different countries was part of the violence and hatred of existing governments spawned by the

   _____ movement.

4. The Russo-Japanese War laid the ground for _____ Sunday, January 9, 1905, when many factory workers and their families were killed.

   There was further revolutionary violence when Tsar _____ appeared to be indifferent to the workers.

5. After Serbia provoked an Austrian ultimatum, Russia began a general mobilization,

   in response to which Germany launched The _____ Plan.

6. During the war in Galicia, Russia lost almost one million men and the countries

   of _____ and _____ .

7. Turkey entered the war in the hope of having some of its territory returned from

   the country of _____ .

8. The Battle of the _____ had a human cost of 1,250,000 dead or wounded.

9. The murder of Rasputin in an attempt to save Russia was accomplished by Felix

   _____ and Vladimir Purishkevich after poisoning, shooting, beating and throwing him into the river.

10. Like his predecessor Nicholas, Alexander _____ continued to allow Russian soldiers to be killed by not withdrawing Russia from the war, so that from March to August 1917, the deserters from the army numbered

_____ million men.

11. The slogan, "Peace, Bread and Land," came from the _____ , the most radical of the revolutionary groups, which _____ immediately took charge of when he arrived in St. Petersburg.

12. Our Lady of Fatima told Lucia, Jacinta and Francisco on July 13, 1917, that if

prayers were offered for the conversion of _____ , it would be converted and peace would be given to the world. If not, that country would spread her errors throughout the world, provoking wars and persecutions of

the _____ .

13. The _____ Revolution on November 7, 1917 began a long and destructive Communist rule. Lenin seized all private property and all Church lands, said that divorce was legal for any reason, and went back on all of his promises about representative government. The royal family was murdered.

Although opposed by forces called the " _____ " in several parts of the country, Communism prevailed.

14. By the time World War I ended on November 11, 1918, _____ ruling families (including the Hapsburgs) had been overthrown, revolution had spread throughout Europe, millions had been killed and a Communist dictatorship had been established in Russia.

Multiple Choice

Directions: After each statement below, there is a set of words or phrases. Circle the letter next to the one word or phrase that best completes the sentence.

1. In 1906, this party was formed under the leadership of David Lloyd George in England:
   - a) Nationalist Party
   - b) Liberal Party
   - c) Traditional Party
   - d) Revolutionary Party

2. The heresy which Pope Pius X condemned, which denied absolute truth and the reliability of the Scriptures, is
      a) Liberalism
      b) Anarchism
      c) Revolutionism
      d) Modernism

3. Tsar Alexander II of Russia, who succeeded Nicholas I, completed all of the following before his assassination except
      a) Trans-Siberian Railroad
      b) Emancipation Act freeing the serfs
      c) establishing idea of Panslavism
      d) establishment of universities
      e) founding of Vladivostok

4. The people greatly respected Nicholas II and Alexandra until they learned of the immoral life of their assistant named
      a) Father George Gapon
      b) Rasputin
      c) Stolypin
      d) none of the above

5. On the evening of August 1, 1914, Germany declared war on Russia and, according to The Schlieffen Plan, invaded
      a) Belgium
      b) France
      c) Austria
      d) Hungary

6. Plan 17 was enacted by this country instead of coming to the aid of the Belgians:
      a) England
      b) United States
      c) France
      d) none of the above

7. All of the following occurred in 1915 except
      a) the German blockade of Great Britain and sinking of the Lusitania
      b) the Austrian/German offensive in Galicia, causing Russia to lose territory
      c) Italy declared war on the Dual Monarchy
      d) Turkey entered the war on Germany's side
      e) Russia made significant progress in the war

8. None of the following were members of the Allies except
      a) England
      b) Germany
      c) Austria-Hungary
      d) Turkey

9. The only ruler willing to surrender his territory and who attempted a secret peace mission known as the "Sixtus Affair" was
   - a) Kaiser Wilhelm
   - b) Nicholas
   - c) Winston Churchill
   - d) Charles of Austria

10. The Nivelle Offensive launched on April 16, 1917 resulted in
    - a) Allied casualties of 120,000
    - b) refusal of duty and desertions in the French army
    - c) replacement of Nivelle with Petain
    - d) b. and c. only
    - e) all of the above

True/False

Directions: Circle the letter T if the statement is true or F if the statement is false.

1. T F The train of thought that Germans were a superior race or "master race" came to Germany with Hitler.

2. T F The first decade of the 20th Century saw stability in Europe.

3. T F Panslavism was the concept of Russian guardianship of all Slavic peoples.

4. T F The Liberals and Radicals were satisfied when Nicholas issued the October Manifesto on October 30, 1905 and established the Duma.

5. T F Before Germany ever declared war on Russia, World War I had its root beginnings in Serbia's provocation of Austria through the assassination of Franz Ferdinand and Sophie.

6. T F Rasputin was an honest and helpful advisor to Nicholas and the Russian government.

7. T F The Germans developed the U-Boats (submarines) as a means of preventing ships from reaching Britain and of establishing a counter-blockade.

8. T F By the end of 1914, both sides in the war had dug into trenches in battle lines that would vary little in the next four years.

9. T F Italy switched to the side of the Allies after England and France made a secret agreement that Italy would receive the South Tyrol from Austria.

10. T   F   General Douglas Haig was a very capable and victorious leader for the Allied Forces, especially at the Battle of the Somme.

11. T   F   The United States entered the war on the side of the Allies.

12. T   F   The Flanders Offensive was bloody but very advantageous to the Allies.

13. T   F   Our Lady of Fatima (Portugal) appeared on May 13, 1917 after Pope Benedict XV's special prayer to the Blessed Mother for peace.

Matching

Directions: This list is made up of names of persons, groups, places and things. Each one corresponds to one of the lettered phrases below. In each blank, write the letter of the phrase that correctly identifies that person, group, place or thing.

1. ___ Queen Victoria

2. ___ Emile Combs

3. ___ Wilhelm II

4. ___ Pope St. Pius X

5. ___ Nicolai Lenin

6. ___ Stolypin

7. ___ Black Hand

8. ___ Gabrilo Princip

9. ___ Alexandra

10. ___ Charles of Austria

11. ___ Zita

12. ___ Sixtus

13. ___ Nivelle

A) founded Russian Social Democrat Labor Party with nine others
B) was a symbol of the British Empire
C) Commander-in-Chief of the French forces
D) murdered Franz Ferdinand and Sophie
E) Germany's militaristic Kaiser

F) succeeded Franz Josef in 1916; was deeply Catholic
G) Nicholas' wife; attributed son's cure to Rasputin
H) violent revolutionary Serbian group
I) France's ruler who oppressed the Church
J) Charles' wife; from Bourbon-Parma family, Italy

K) condemned Modernism and appealed for peace
L) Zita's brother—Charles' secret peace mission
M) Nicholas' prime minister—land reform program

Mini-Essay Question: Briefly name some of the effects of World War I on history.
(Extra credit—4 points.)

Personal Opinion: Name an important or interesting fact that you learned in this chapter. How could this fact affect your life?

Supplemental Reading

F. A. Forbes. *Pope St. Pius X.* TAN.

Msgr. Joseph A. Cirrincione. *Ven. Francisco Marto of Fatima.* (Booklet). TAN.

Msgr. Joseph A. Cirrincione. *Ven. Jacinta Marto of Fatima.* (Booklet). TAN.

Mary Fabyan Windeatt. *The Children of Fatima.* TAN.

THE WORLD BETWEEN WARS

Perfect Score: 100
(Each Question is worth 2 points.)

Score: _____

Completion

Directions: Complete and make each statement true and accurate by writing one or more words on each blank line.

1. U.S. President Woodrow Wilson refused to speak to Charles of Austria regarding peace negotiations because of his (Wilson's) prejudice against governments that had not been _____ . President Wilson's _____ , a list of conditions that he thought should be included in any peace treaty, also supported the destruction of the Austrian Empire.

2. The one beneficial aspect of the Versailles Treaty was that Germany, Austria, and Russia gave back territory for the country of _____ .

3. Two primary effects of the Versailles Treaty were the bitterness of the _____ and the destruction of the _____ .

4. The last Hapsburg Emperor, _____ , lived such a holy life that the Church began investigation into his possible canonization.

5. Despite Wilson's touring the country for public support for the _____ , the U.S. never joined.

6. Hitler used the constitution of Germany to obtain his dictatorship legally by the passing of the _____ Act, which allowed a Chancellor to rule by decree.

7. Hitler stated that he would conquer all of Europe and then turn on his greatest enemy, the _____ .

8. In the first third of the 20th century, when the atheist Azana came to power in Spain, he closed Catholic schools, removed religious symbols from public buildings and expelled the _____ .

9. Under Azana's rule, Spain became a divided nation. The two groups were the revolutionaries, who were known as _____ and the traditionalists who were known as _____ .

10. The Spaniards felt deeply that their rising against the Communist government (Spanish Civil War) was a holy war, so it came to be called the _____ or Crusade.

11. Spain lost two-thirds of its entire _____ reserve to Communist Russia in exchange for arms, technicians, trainers and officers which the revolutionaries used to try to defeat the traditionalists.

12. The battle which best symbolizes the issues of the three-year Spanish Civil War is the Siege of the _____ in Toledo. This battle demonstrated the courage and character of the traditionalists.

13. Spain did not assist the Allies in World War II; after the War, the civilized world turned against Spain and refused to provide any _____ or _____ , allowing many Spanish to starve to death.

14. The Spanish Civil War is so important in 20th-century history because in Spain the _____ suffered a decisive defeat after having apparently achieved a complete victory.

Multiple Choice

Directions: After each statement below, there is a set of words or phrases. Circle the letter next to the one word or phrase that best completes the sentence.

1. At the Versailles Conference after World War I, President Woodrow Wilson supported
   a) self-determination
   b) establishment of the United Nations
   c) establishment of the League of Nations
   d) a. and c.
   e) all of the above

2. Part of Yugoslavia's problem, after Wilson redrew the map of Europe, was that two groups that intensely disliked each other were united in the same country. These groups are the
   - a) Slovaks and Croats
   - b) Serbs and Croats
   - c) Slovaks and Serbs
   - d) none of the above

3. The Allies' punishment of Germany through the Versailles Treaty included all of the following except
   - a) return of Alsace and Lorraine to France
   - b) payment of reparations to Allies
   - c) limits on guns and warships, destruction of tanks and airplanes
   - d) smaller nations within Germany given independence
   - e) Allies occupied the Rhineland

4. In addition to the millions of Russians who died during World War I, Russian deaths by starvation when Communism under Lenin failed totaled
   - a) three million
   - b) four million
   - c) five million
   - d) six million

5. Lenin's attacks on family life in Russia included all of the following except
   - a) collective farms
   - b) abortion available on demand
   - c) children were encouraged to spy on their parents
   - d) marriage and divorce by signing a government register
   - e) children were indoctrinated in Communism

6. After the war, many people felt that liberal, democratic, parliamentary systems just did not work because of the problems these systems had led to in
   - a) England
   - b) Spain
   - c) France
   - d) Italy
   - e) all of the above

7. A Fascist government worked to the benefit of Portugal. Which of the following countries also benefited from a pro-Christian fascist government?
   - a) Portugal
   - b) Italy
   - c) Romania
   - d) a. and c.
   - e) all of the above

8. The Popular Front, which won the 1936 election in Spain, was a combination of leftist groups who the traditionalists referred to as
        a) Caballero
        b) The Front
        c) The Reds
        d) none of the above

9. The Spanish Civil War lasted from
        a) 1916–1919
        b) 1926–1929
        c) 1936–1939
        d) 1946–1949

10. The restoration of order, peace and prosperity in Spain under the leadership of Franco lasted for a period of over
        a) 25 years
        b) 30 years
        c) 35 years
        d) none of the above

True/False

Directions: Circle the letter T if the statement is true or F if the statement is false.

1.   T   F   England and France were eager to establish the League of Nations to guarantee world peace.

2.   T   F   Wilson wanted to impose the American form of government on the rest of the world.

3.   T   F   Wilson redrew the map of Europe, putting Czechs and Slovaks, who did not get along, into Czechoslovakia, and giving Austria's South Tyrol to Italy after believing the lie that it was part of "historic" Italy.

4.   T   F   After the war, Charles fled to Switzerland while Austria's six and a half century empire was divided without his consultation.

5.   T   F   The Germans were supposed to pay the Allies five billion dollars in reparations, due in five years, as a requirement of the Versailles Treaty.

6.   T   F   Without the protection of the Hapsburg Empire, the newly created small nations' independence survived only twenty years. They were conquered by the Nazis and the Communists.

7.   T   F   Charles of Austria tried to regain the throne in Hungary but was betrayed by one of his own generals, along with others who should have been his supporters.

8.   T   F   The United States joined the League of Nations in 1921.

9.   T   F   Lenin's New Economic Policy of 1922 put ownership of manufacturing and farming strictly in the hands of the government and discouraged foreign capitalism.

10.   T   F   Stalin's purges were a series of arrests, trials and executions of persons known to have opposed Communism.

11.   T   F   Fascism means a government without elections, but with a parliament and one strong head of state.

12.   T   F   Hitler obtained his dictatorial powers legally in accord with the German constitution.

13.   T   F   Of the 1,760 people who were in the Alcazar only 92 soldiers died. No women or any of the 211 children died.

Matching

Directions: This list is made up of names of persons, groups, places and things. Each one corresponds to one of the lettered phrases below. In each blank, write the letter of the phrase that correctly identifies that person, group, place or thing.

1. ___ Pres. Clemenceau

2. ___ Lloyd George

3. ___ Polish Corridor

4. ___ Madeira

5. ___ collective farm

6. ___ Benito Mussolini

7. ___ Blackshirts

8. ___ Lateran Treaty

9. ___ Pope Pius XI

10. ___ *Mein Kampf*

11. ___ Reichstag

12. ___ *Mit Brennender Sorge*

13. ___ Requetes

A) peasants placed on government owned land
B) "With Burning Sorrow"—condemned Nazism
C) outlet to the sea that was cut through Germany
D) condemned the Fascists for their pagan values
E) granted the Pope Vatican City
F) France's ruler
G) military arm of the Carlists
H) *My Struggle*; written by Hitler
I) Great Britain's Prime Minister
J) Germany's Parliament
K) Charles and his family were driven into exile to this island
L) Fascist ruler of Italy
M) nickname for the Italian Fascist Party

Mini-Essay Question:
(Extra credit—4 points.)

List the two areas where Franco is criticized and give a defense of his position on each.

Personal Opinion:

Name an important or interesting fact that you learned in this chapter. How could this fact affect your life?

Supplemental Reading

Dr. Warren H. Carroll. *The Last Crusade*. (On the Spanish Civil War). Christendom Press.

Perfect Score: 100
(Each Question is worth 2 points.)

Score: _____

Completion

Directions: Complete and make each statement true and accurate by writing one or more words on each blank line.

1. Hitler's goal of uniting all German-speaking people of Europe included the conquest of Czechoslovakia because of the three and one-fourth million Germans who lived in an area known as the _____ .

2. The Munich conference between Chamberlain and Hitler is a prime example of _____ , a policy of allowing dictators to have their way.

3. Hitler's third target was the country of _____ , to which Prime Minister Chamberlain guaranteed independence.

4. Thousands of Poles were deported to slave labor camps after the Communists murdered ten thousand Polish army officers in the _____ Forest Massacre.

5. The British people actually saved their army by responding quickly when the government called for the evacuation of troops from the Port of _____ (on the Belgium coast).

6. For 57 nights the Germans spent their time bombing London; this is known as the _____ , and it gave the Royal Air Force time to get ready for war.

7. The Japanese bombing of the U.S. fleet in Pearl Harbor on _____ took place because Japan saw the U.S. as its primary rival in the Pacific.

8. The U.S. and Japan both had so many warships sunk off Guadalcanal in the Solomon Islands that its waters were called _____ Bay.

9. At Stalingrad (in South Russia), 280,000 men lost their lives because Hitler refused to listen to General _____ .

10. With the British and American invasion of _____ on November 8, 1943, the Allies finally took the offensive.

11. American and British pilots attempted to terrorize Germany into ending the war by bombing the homes and working places of its civilians. This is known as _____ bombing.

12. Communist leaders wanted to dominate the countries of _____ after the war. Churchill and Roosevelt agreed to give Stalin a free hand there in exchange for his cooperation.

13. The Philippines were regained by the U.S. in the Battle of _____ Gulf on October 20, 1944 under General MacArthur, who kept his promise to the American and Filipino people.

14. Father _____ —who has since been canonized—voluntarily took the place of a married man with children to die in a _____ bunker at Auschwitz.

Multiple Choice

Directions: After each statement below, there is a set of words or phrases. Circle the letter next to the one word or phrase that best completes the sentence.

1. Hitler violated the Versailles Treaty by
   a) building up his army and navy
   b) failing to make reparations
   c) occupying the Rhineland
   d) failing to return Alsace and Lorraine to France
   e) a. and c.
   f) b. and d.

2. The Axis Powers included all of the following except
   a) Germany
   b) Italy
   c) France
   d) Japan

3. The agreement between Germany and the USSR to prevent war between each other was called
       a) appeasement
       b) the New Order
       c) Co-prosperity Pact
       d) the Ribbentrop Pact

4. The period of months after the September 1939 invasion of Poland by Germany, when there was little action except the blocking of German ports by Great Britain, even though France and England had declared war, is known as the
       a) Sitzkrieg
       b) Blitzkrieg
       c) Blitz
       d) none of the above

5. The French Resistance Movement (to fight Nazi occupation) formed after Hitler signed a treaty with
       a) George Patton
       b) Pinchas Lapids
       c) Winston Churchill
       d) Marshal Petain

6. The air war between the Luftwaffe and the RAF was known as the
       a) Battle of the Bulge
       b) Battle of Britain
       c) Battle of the Coral Sea
       d) Battle of the Ardennes Forest

7. Hitler's invasion of Russia was to be accomplished through his plan known as
       a) Operation Punishment
       b) Operation Russia
       c) Operation Barbarossa
       d) Operation Moscow

8. The secret agents who smuggled out of Poland one of the Germans' code machines were
       a) British
       b) French
       c) American
       d) Russian

9. On December 12, 1944, the Germans attacked through the Ardennes Forest in the bloody battle known as the
       a) Battle of the Bulge
       b) Battle of Britain
       c) Battle of the Coral Sea
       d) Battle of the Ardennes Forest

10. The first atomic bomb dropped on Japan, which killed more than 100,000 civilians, was dropped on

        a) Nagasaki

        b) Iwo Jima

        c) Okinawa

        d) Hiroshima

True/False

Directions: Circle the letter T if the statement is true or F if the statement is false.

1.   T   F   The first target of Hitler in his goal to unite the German-speaking people was the country of Austria, which he absorbed with no action from Great Britain or France.

2.   T   F   Poland was overcome by Hitler's army through the lightning war known as the Sitzkrieg.

3.   T   F   After declaring war against Germany on September 3, 1939, England and France sent assistance to the Poles, but Germany still prevailed.

4.   T   F   The best-kept secret of the war, which was revealed in 1974, was the Ultra.

5.   T   F   After breaking through the Maginot line and occupying Paris, Hitler took revenge upon France, forcing Petain to sign the surrender treaty in the same spot where Germany had surrendered after World War I.

6.   T   F   Hitler relied on his Luftwaffe to soften up Britain for his planned invasion of England which he called Operation Sea Lion.

7.   T   F   The first retreat of the Germans during the war was at the Battle of the Bulge against the Americans.

8.   T   F   The Japanese fighter planes which attacked the Yorktown and other American carriers at Midway Island were called the Torpedoes.

9.   T   F   The *Washington* was the battleship used by the Americans in the decisive battle which they won against the Japanese at Guadalcanal.

10.   T   F   D-Day refers to the invasion of Allied troops on the shore of Normandy, France.

11.   T   F   Britain and America announced that the Allies would only negotiate a peace treaty with a German leader other than Hitler.

12.   T   F   Although the Americans wanted to arrange peace terms, the Japanese wanted to continue the war.

13.   T   F   The extermination of millions of Jews and others was carried out by the Nazis at the extermination camps of Belsen, Dachau, Auschwitz and others.

Matching

Directions: This list is made up of names of persons, groups, places and things. Each one corresponds to one of the lettered phrases below. In each blank, write the letter of the phrase that correctly identifies that person, group, place or thing.

1. ___ Schuschnigg

2. ___ Neville Chamberlain

3. ___ Winston Churchill

4. ___ Marshal Petain

5. ___ Hermann Goering

6. ___ Tojo

7. ___ Douglas MacArthur

8. ___ Raymond Spruance

9. ___ Dwight Eisenhower

10. ___ Von Stauffenberg

11. ___ George Patton

12. ___ Dr. Zolli

13. ___ Pinchas Lapids

A) head of the Luftwaffe
B) attempted Hitler's assassination
C) General—directed Allied invasion of North Africa
D) Chief Rabbi of Rome; became Catholic after the war
E) agreed to German domination of the Sudetenland

F) commanded U.S. Naval victory at Midway Island
G) Japan's Prime Minister; ordered attack on U.S.
H) General—tank commander of Allied forces
I) forced to give Nazis control of Austrian government
J) Premier of France

K) commander of Allied forces in Southwest Pacific
L) Jewish leader and Israeli Consul in Italy
M) British Prime Minister through most of World War II

Mini-Essay Question:
(Extra credit—4 points.)

List three reasons which clearly show that Pope Pius XII (either personally or through others) was working to protect the Jews against the Nazis during World War II.

Personal Opinion:

Name an important or interesting fact that you learned in this chapter. How could this fact affect your life?

Supplemental Reading

Fr. Jeremiah J. Smith, O.F.M. Conv. *Saint Maximilian Kolbe: Knight of the Immaculata.* TAN.

Perfect Score: 100
(Each Question is worth 2 points.)

Score: _____

Completion

Directions: Complete and make each statement true and accurate by writing one or more words on each blank line.

1. The Yalta Conference was attended by U.S. President Franklin Roosevelt, British Prime Minister _____ and Soviet dictator

   _____ .

2. The Truman Doctrine, or _____ , advocated the supplying of aid to countries when the Communists threatened to take over.

3. The civil war in China that lasted more than twenty years between the

   Communists and the _____ resulted in a victory for Communism in October of 1949, after the failure of the U.S. government to provide substantial aid to the anti-Communist forces in that country.

4. The U.S. government did not take Communism seriously at first, preferring

   to dismiss the issue until forced to take action. The _____ War was a high point of the Cold War in that whole struggle.

5. When Nagy re-assumed power, he stood firm against the Soviet Union; he prepared the declarations of Hungary's neutrality and of its leaving the

   _____ Pact.

6. The United States, under President _____ , refused to assist the Hungarian Freedom Fighters in their 1956 struggle against Communism, giving the reason that U.S. or U.N. units could not help Hungary without traversing neutral territory.

7. The Communists overtook the island of _____ in January of 1960.

8. Although that island failed to regain its freedom, the countries of

   _____ and _____ overthrew their Communist governments in 1964 and 1973, respectively.

9. The U.S. bears much responsibility for the collapse of the South Vietnamese government under Catholic leader _____ .

10. In 1975 the Communists launched a major offensive, gaining control of several countries; their only failure in 1975 was in the country of _____ , where the Communists were forced out through Our Lady of Fatima's intercession.

11. Finally, in the mid-1980's under President _____ , the United States began supporting freedom fighters with aid.

12. After Poland, Germany, Czechoslovakia, Hungary and the other republics of the U.S.S.R. proclaimed their independence, _____ was elected President of the Russian Republic on June 12, 1991.

13. In a 20-year period (from 1965-1985), the Catholic population of _____ went from 29 million to 66 million, with South Korea, Poland and Central and South America also showing great increases.

14. In the 20th century, the greatest internal threat to the Church has probably been the heresy of _____ , while the greatest external threat has been _____ .

Multiple Choice

Directions: After each statement below, there is a set of words or phrases. Circle the letter next to the one word or phrase that best completes the sentence.

1. The Communists attempted to extend their influence over which of these countries by starting civil wars in 1947:
    a) Greece and Turkey
    b) Greece and Italy
    c) Turkey and Italy
    d) none of the above

2. The question of territories conquered by Russia and Japan during World War II was settled by the
    a) Truman Doctrine
    b) Yalta Conference
    c) Cold War
    d) none of the above

3. The liberal counterattack on Senator McCarthy included accusing McCarthy of which of the following:

    a) creating a "climate of fear"
    b) suppressing free speech
    c) "character assassination"
    d) insanity
    e) all of the above

4. On November 4, 1956, when the Russians issued an order to "conquer or exterminate" the Freedom Fighters, thirty-two students formed a barricade around a statue of this saint, the Patron Saint of Hungarian youth:

    a) St. Hermenegild
    b) St. Sebastian
    c) St. John Bosco
    d) St. Imre

5. What percent of Hungarians were Catholic at the time of the 1956 Freedom uprising?

    a) 50%
    b) 60%
    c) 75%
    d) 85%

6. Nixon's policy of *detente* included which of the following ideas:

    a) there are no significant differences between Communist and Western countries
    b) Communist and Western countries should cooperate wherever possible
    c) Communist and Western countries should no longer regard themselves as enemies
    d) a. and c. only
    e) all of the above

7. Mikhail Gorbachev, the General Secretary of the Communist Party, in 1986 allowed the Eastern European countries to depart from Communism through his policies of

    a) solidarity and glasnost
    b) solidarity and perestroika
    c) glasnost and counter-revolution
    d) glasnost and perestroika
    e) counter-revolution and solidarity

8. The first session of Vatican Council II was called by Pope

    a) John XXIII
    b) Pius XI
    c) Pius XII
    d) Paul VI

9. Vatican Council II lasted from
        a) 1968–1972
        b) 1957–1960
        c) 1970–1975
        d) 1962–1965

10. Pope John Paul II (Karol Wojtyla of Poland), who became Pope in 1978, accomplished all of the following in the first few years of his pontificate except
        a) continued strong moral teaching
        b) began to discipline Modernist leaders
        c) traveled extensively around the world
        d) wrote the encyclical *Humanae Vitae*

True/False

Directions: Circle the letter T if the statement is true or F if the statement is false.

1.   T   F   The "Big Three" refers to the three major conferences held after the war.

2.   T   F   The Berlin Blockade refers to the halting of all rail and road traffic into West Berlin by the Communists in July of 1948.

3.   T   F   The Cold War means opposition by the United States to Communism and to the increasing of power or territories by the Soviet Union.

4.   T   F   After the Marine landing at Inchon, MacArthur spread U.S. troops in North Korea too thinly, assuming that the war would be won quickly.

5.   T   F   Colonel Pal Maleter (a Communist) was sent into Hungary from Russia to stop the rebellion of the Hungarian Freedom Fighters in the army barracks, but instead he joined them, so impressed was he by their courage and their conviction.

6.   T   F   When the U.S. remained committed to the policy of containment, the independence of Greece and Turkey was safeguarded.

7.   T   F   After the Chinese emperor was overthrown in 1912, two leaders emerged: Mao Tse-tung, a Christian anti-Communist, and Chiang Kai-shek, a Communist.

8.   T   F   At the Geneva Conferences, Laos and South Vietnam were given their independence, but Cambodia and North Vietnam became Communist.

9.   T   F   Nixon essentially allowed North Vietnamese Communists to take over South Vietnam by withdrawing U.S. troops but allowing the North Vietnamese to remain.

10.   T   F   Mikhail Gorbachev allowed the people of Eastern Europe to choose freedom, and one after another, beginning with Czechoslovakia, they did.

11.   T   F   Modernism is the heresy that denies the historical reliability of Scripture, says that the Incarnation is not a fact and claims that there is no absolute, unchanging truth.

12.   T   F   Pope Paul VI did not discipline the Modernist leaders, but he upheld orthodoxy through clear teaching; this policy earned him criticism from both sides.

13.   T   F   In the Western world, the sundering of Christendom in the 16th century led to the moral corruption of the late 20th century.

Matching

Directions: This list is made up of names of persons, groups, places and things. Each one corresponds to one of the lettered phrases below. In each blank, write the letter of the phrase that correctly identifies that person, group, place or thing.

1. ___   Alger Hiss

2. ___   Konrad Adenauer

3. ___   Mao Tse-tung

4. ___   Chiang Kai-shek

5. ___   Whittaker Chambers

6. ___   Joseph McCarthy

7. ___   Erno Gero

8. ___   Imre Nagy

9. ___   Eisenhower

10. ___   Ho Chi Minh

11. ___   Ngo Dinh Diem

12. ___   Francisco Maria da Silva

13. ___   Lech Walesa

A) leader of Hungary during Freedom Fighters uprising

B) refused aid to Hungarian Freedom Fighters

C) former Communist; wrote the book *Witness*

D) Communist leader in Vietnam

E) tried to prove Communist infiltration in army

F) Catholic South Vietnamese government leader

G) led Solidarity—Catholic labor union movement in Poland

H) Archbishop of Braga; spiritual inspiration against Communism in Portugal

I) Communist leader; fought Freedom Fighters

J) leader of the Chinese Communists

K) leader of Chinese Christian Nationalist forces

L) Communist advisor to Roosevelt

M) able leader of West Germany after World War II

Mini-Essay Question:
(Extra credit—4 points.)
Why was it unjust for the leaders of England and the U.S. to turn Poland over to Russia after World War II?

Personal Opinion:
Name an important or interesting fact that you learned in this chapter. How could this fact affect your life?

Supplemental Reading

Dr. Warren H. Carroll. *The Rise and Fall of the Communist Revolution*. Christendom Press.

Fr. J. B. Lemius, O.M.I. *A Catechism of Moderism*. TAN.

Fr. Ralph Wiltgen, S.V.D. *The Rhine Flows into the Tiber: A History of Vatican II*. TAN.

ANSWER KEY

Chapter 1: WHAT HISTORY IS ALL ABOUT (Pages 7-12)

Completion
1. record; events
2. historians
3. historian; point of view
4. historical
5. Incarnation
6. where
7. achievements; effect
8. Before Christ
9. Year of Our Lord
10. B.C.
11. 2000
12. prehistoric
13. the Bible
14. Hebrew

Multiple Choice
1. d   6. c
2. d   7. c
3. c   8. b
4. f   9. a
5. b   10. b

True/False
1. F   8. F
2. F   9. T
3. F   10. T
4. T   11. T
5. T   12. T
6. F   13. T
7. F

Matching
1. C   8. A
2. D   9. H
3. F   10. E
4. K   11. J
5. B   12. G
6. M   13. I
7. L

Mini-Essay Question. The Catholic Bible includes the Books originally written in both Hebrew and Greek, whereas the Protestant Bible only includes the Books originally written in Hebrew.

Chapter 2: ABRAHAM (Pages 15-23)

Completion
1. Neolithic Revolution; population
2. cities; writing
3. government; trade
4. Sumerians
5. Suttee
6. reincarnation
7. covenant
8. Europe; Africa
9. fidelity; trust
10. obeyed
11. complete; Isaac
12. billion
13. mosque
14. Joseph

Multiple Choice
1. b   6. b
2. a   7. e
3. d   8. a
4. c   9. c
5. d   10. e

True/False
1. T   8. F
2. F   9. F
3. T   10. F
4. F   11. F
5. F   12. T
6. F   13. T
7. T

Matching
1. D   8. E
2. A   9. J
3. G   10. C
4. B   11. M
5. I   12. H
6. L   13. F
7. K

Mini-Essay Question. He had complete trust in God. Also, he was willing to do God's Will without hesitation.

Chapter 3: MOSES (Pages 25-30)

Completion
1. Seti I; Rameses II
2. self-existent
3. plagues
4. natural; nature
5. journey
6. sin
7. cloud; fire
8. complain; providence
9. oasis
10. priests
11. Ten Commandments
12. blood sacrifice
13. prayer
14. Joshua; Caleb

Multiple Choice
1. b   6. c
2. d   7. b
3. c   8. d
4. a   9. b
5. d   10. a

True/False
1. F   8. T
2. T   9. F
3. T   10. T
4. F   11. F
5. T   12. F
6. T   13. T
7. T

Matching
1. J   8. F
2. H   9. C
3. E   10. D
4. G   11. A
5. I   12. M
6. K   13. L
7. B

Mini-Essay Question. The Passover foreshadowed the day when God would free all men from the slavery of sin through the shedding of the Blood of His own Son, Jesus Christ, who was called the Lamb of God.

Chapter 4: THE KINGDOM OF ISRAEL (Pages 32-41)

Completion

1. Joshua
2. king
3. David
4. Jerusalem
5. king
6. faithful; do evil
7. happiness
8. Israel; Judah
9. Mount Carmel
10. Elias
11. prophets
12. Isaias
13. Ezechiel
14. Chosen People

Multiple Choice

1.	b	6.	e
2.	b	7.	b
3.	a	8.	b
4.	b	9.	c
5.	a	10.	b

True/False

1.	F	8.	T
2.	T	9.	T
3.	F	10.	F
4.	F	11.	F
5.	T	12.	T
6.	F	13.	T
7.	T		

Matching

1.	K	8.	M
2.	D	9.	G
3.	A	10.	J
4.	L	11.	C
5.	B	12.	E
6.	I	13.	H
7.	F		

Mini-Essay Question. He may have been a Zoroastrian, in which case he believed in an all-powerful Creator-God who loves right and abhors wrong, and who rewards good and punishes evil.

Chapter 5: THE ACHIEVEMENT OF GREECE (Pages 43-50)

Completion

1. city-states
2. Marathon
3. Sparta
4. Golden Age
5. Euclid; Hippocrates
6. philosophy
7. answers; solutions
8. Europe
9. rationally; reason
10. Alexander
11. Aristotle
12. end; world
13. Roxana
14. Ptolemaic Egypt; Seleucid Syria

Multiple Choice

1.	c	6.	b
2.	a	7.	c
3.	a	8.	b
4.	c	9.	d
5.	d	10.	e

True/False

1.	T	8.	T
2.	F	9.	F
3.	F	10.	T
4.	T	11.	T
5.	T	12.	T
6.	T	13.	T
7.	F		

Matching

1.	C	8.	D
2.	L	9.	B
3.	G	10.	H
4.	J	11.	A
5.	K	12.	E
6.	F	13.	I
7.	M		

Mini-Essay Question. The Persian Wars stopped the expansion of Persia and marked the beginning of the West, where Christian civilization would be built. The lands penetrated by Greek culture would become Christian.

Chapter 6: THE ACHIEVEMENT OF ROME (Pages 52-65)

Completion

1. maniples
2. citizenship
3. consuls
4. tribunes
5. natural law
6. Punic
7. Sicily
8. Scipio
9. salt
10. Popillius
11. monotheists; polytheists
12. Social
13. First Triumvirate
14. philosophy

Multiple Choice

1.	b	6.	b
2.	e	7.	a
3.	b	8.	a
4.	d	9.	a
5.	a	10.	c

True/False

1.	F	8.	F
2.	T	9.	T
3.	T	10.	T
4.	T	11.	F
5.	F	12.	T
6.	T	13.	T
7.	T		

Matching

1.	M	8.	C
2.	A	9.	F
3.	H	10.	I
4.	J	11.	D
5.	B	12.	K
6.	L	13.	G
7.	E		

Mini-Essay Question.
1. The defeat of Carthage.
2. Natural Law Philosophy.
3. The spread of civilization into western and northern Europe.
4. A period of peace and order.

Chapter 7: THE MOST IMPORTANT EVENT IN HISTORY (Pages 67-78)

Completion

1. New Testament
2. closeness
3. four
4. Infancy
5. Jordan
6. Law
7. psychologically
8. naturalistic
9. four
10. three
11. Heart
12. linen
13. Pontius Pilate
14. Resurrection; undisturbed

Multiple Choice

1.	d	6.	b
2.	c	7.	c
3.	b	8.	c
4.	e	9.	e
5.	a	10.	d

True/False

1.	T	8.	F
2.	T	9.	F
3.	F	10.	F
4.	F	11.	T
5.	F	12.	T
6.	T	13.	T
7.	F		

Matching

1.	C	8.	B
2.	K	9.	M
3.	I	10.	H
4.	F	11.	J
5.	L	12.	E
6.	A	13.	G
7.	D		

Mini-Essay Question.

1) Contamination—The Shroud was touched by many people and articles over the centuries.
2) The fire in the Chambery Church in 1532 which housed the Shroud—both the air-tight tube and the intense heat could have altered the test results.
3) The event which probably produced the image—the Resurrection—could have had an impact on the test [by altering the Shroud in some way].

[Editor's note: Research since 1988 has provided much additional evidence of flaws in the 1988 Carbon 14 test.]

Chapter 8: THE APOSTOLIC AGE (Pages 80-89)

Completion

1. Peter
2. Jews
3. St. Stephen; Damascus
4. Gentiles
5. Jerusalem
6. Mesopotamia; India
7. Edessa
8. Face
9. Chrestus
10. Christians
11. beheading
12. four
13. Patmos; Revelation (or the Apocalypse)
14. Rome; Temple

Multiple Choice

1.	a	6.	b
2.	b	7.	c
3.	c	8.	a
4.	d	9.	e
5.	d	10.	b

True/False

1.	F	8.	F
2.	T	9.	F
3.	T	10.	T
4.	T	11.	F
5.	F	12.	T
6.	F	13.	T
7.	T		

Matching

1.	E	8.	D
2.	J	9.	L
3.	G	10.	I
4.	M	11.	H
5.	C	12.	F
6.	A	13.	K
7.	B		

Mini-Essay Question.
Rome was the leading city of the world. Decisions made there affected the lives of people throughout the civilized world. Everyone looked to Rome for leadership. Therefore it was essential that the headquarters of the Church be located in Rome.

Chapter 9: EMPIRE VERSUS CHURCH (Pages 91-100)

Completion

1. 20
2. Christians
3. martyrs
4. Nicomedia
5. collapse
6. Galerius; Romula
7. 1600
8. ulcer
9. cross
10. Christ
11. Milvian
12. Toleration
13. neutral
14. Christendom

Multiple Choice

1.	a	6.	c
2.	c	7.	d
3.	b	8.	b
4.	e	9.	a
5.	b	10.	a

True/False

1.	T	8.	F
2.	F	9.	T
3.	F	10.	F
4.	F	11.	T
5.	T	12.	T
6.	T	13.	T
7.	T		

Matching

1.	E	8.	M
2.	J	9.	C
3.	A	10.	K
4.	L	11.	I
5.	H	12.	F
6.	B	13.	D
7.	G		

Mini-Essay Question.
Constantine modified the Roman laws to reflect Christian principles. He is honored as the Founder of Christendom.

Chapter 10: THE GREAT HERESIES   (Pages 102-116)

Completion

1. Constantinople
2. East
3. being
4. Nicene Creed
5. Liberius
6. Athanasius
7. Apostate
8. Sacrifice; Mass
9. Ambrose
10. grace
11. Ephesus
12. garment
13. Tome
14. Theodora

Multiple Choice

1. c	6. e
2. a	7. a
3. b	8. c
4. b	9. d
5. d	10. d

True/False

1. T	8. F
2. F	9. T
3. T	10. F
4. F	11. F
5. T	12. T
6. T	13. F
7. T	

Matching

1. D	8. E
2. J	9. H
3. G	10. I
4. L	11. C
5. A	12. K
6. B	13. F
7. M	

Mini-Essay Question.   Jesus was one divine Person with two natures, human and divine. As a mother is the mother of a person, not of a nature alone, Mary is the mother of a divine Person; therefore, she deserves the title "Mother of God."

Chapter 11: THE BARBARIANS AND THE CHURCH   (Pages 118-131)

Completion

1. Christianity
2. Goths
3. Leo
4. Golden Age
5. Book
6. Colmcille
7. Brendan
8. England; Europe
9. study; work
10. Catholic
11. queen
12. Reccared
13. Rome
14. Canterbury

Multiple Choice

1. a	6. e
2. d	7. a
3. b	8. b
4. b	9. d
5. a	10. c

True/False

1. T	8. F
2. F	9. T
3. F	10. T
4. T	11. T
5. T	12. F
6. T	13. T
7. F	

Matching

1. D	8. E
2. F	9. J
3. H	10. M
4. I	11. G
5. B	12. C
6. K	13. A
7. L	

Mini-Essay Question.   The monasteries were centers of learning, growing or making everything needed and preserving knowledge of craftsmanship and agriculture which would have been lost. They preserved what was best from the old Roman civilization. They were centers of order, peace, self-discipline and beauty amidst the war, hatred and selfishness (disorder) of the barbarism outside.

Chapter 12: THE PROPHET AND THE EMPEROR   (Pages 133-142)

Completion

1. Ctesiphon
2. Koran
3. Islam; Moslem
4. army
5. three
6. Christ; Spain
7. Franks
8. Byzantium
9. Lombards
10. Papal States
11. conversion
12. Carolingian
13. Holy
14. Builder

Multiple Choice

1. b	6. c
2. a	7. b
3. d	8. c
4. c	9. e
5. e	10. c

True/False

1. T	8. T
2. T	9. T
3. F	10. F
4. F	11. F
5. F	12. F
6. F	13. T
7. T	

Matching

1. C	8. K
2. G	9. D
3. A	10. F
4. M	11. L
5. J	12. E
6. I	13. H
7. B	

Mini-Essay Question.   The Carolingian Age was a Golden Age which flourished under Charlemagne in France during the last quarter of the eighth century. The arts and education flourished. Painters, silversmiths, goldsmiths, ivory carvers, manuscript illuminators, sculptors and scholars received Charlemagne's support. Schools were established by the monk Alcuin. Good roads were built. Just government and enforcement of justice were established.

Chapter 13: THE FOUNDATION OF A NEW CIVILIZATION (Pages 144-157)

Completion

1. Dark Ages
2. three
3. Verdun
4. France; Germany
5. warriors
6. Alfred
7. England
8. feudalism
9. Saxony
10. Corpse
11. Odo
12. Slavonic; Bulgars
13. faith; morals
14. Constantinople

Multiple Choice

1.	b	6.	d
2.	c	7.	d
3.	a	8.	b
4.	b	9.	a
5.	c	10.	c

True/False

1.	T	8.	T
2.	F	9.	T
3.	F	10.	T
4.	T	11.	F
5.	F	12.	T
6.	F	13.	T
7.	F		

Matching

1.	G	8.	E
2.	C	9.	K
3.	L	10.	F
4.	I	11.	H
5.	M	12.	B
6.	A	13.	D
7.	J		

Mini-Essay Question. During the 10 years of peace in Ireland beginning in 1002, when Brian Boru was crowned High King, roads, bridges, harbors and fortresses were built. Monasteries, churches, schools and colleges were endowed. Complete order and peace were established (as shown, for example, in the story of the richly dressed girl who walked the length of Ireland without trouble).

Chapter 14: THE HIGH MIDDLE AGES (Pages 159-180)

Completion

1. Holy Roman Empire; feudal system
2. Lithuanians; 1400
3. simony; celibacy
4. Urban II; Clermont
5. Moslems
6. Jerusalem
7. Knights of St. John; Hospitallers
8. St. Bernard
9. papal authority
10. Constantinople
11. *perfecti*; license to sin
12. Preachers; Third
13. Simon de Montfort
14. Inquisition

Multiple Choice

1.	c	6.	b
2.	a	7.	b
3.	d	8.	e
4.	d	9.	c
5.	a	10.	c

True/False

1.	F	8.	F
2.	F	9.	T
3.	T	10.	F
4.	F	11.	F
5.	T	12.	F
6.	T	13.	F
7.	T		

Matching

1.	G	8.	C
2.	J	9.	E
3.	M	10.	H
4.	A	11.	L
5.	B	12.	I
6.	K	13.	F
7.	D		

Mini-Essay Question.

(See p. 164 in *Christ the King—Lord of History*)

Any two of the following:

1. The Moslems had been aggressors against the Christians since the seventh century, and their attacks on Christian countries were still going on in the eleventh century.
2. In 1071 the Turks had attacked and virtually annihilated the Byzantine army at Manzikert.
3. The Christian countries of Europe were going on the offensive in order to prevent future attacks.
4. At no point did the Crusaders attack the Moslem homeland, Arabia, but only those originally Christian territories that the Moslems had conquered.

Chapter 15: THE GREATEST OF CENTURIES   (Pages 182-200)

Completion

1. IX
2. Frederick II
3. God
4. reason; truths
5. Transubstantiation
6. journeymen; master
7. chivalry
8. St. Albert the Great; Roger Bacon
9. Babylonian Captivity
10. France
11. Catholicism
12. Black Death
13. 1453
14. Hungary

Multiple Choice

1.	b	6.	d
2.	e	7.	a
3.	a	8.	c
4.	b	9.	a
5.	c	10.	e

True/False

1.	T	8.	T
2.	T	9.	F
3.	F	10.	F
4.	F	11.	T
5.	F	12.	T
6.	F	13.	T
7.	F		

Matching

1.	J	8.	E
2.	D	9.	G
3.	L	10.	I
4.	B	11.	F
5.	H	12.	K
6.	A	13.	C
7.	M		

Mini-Essay Question. Because only God is self-existent, He is the source of all being. Therefore all being is good. The material world, the body and procreation must be respected as coming from God and hallowed by God's assuming a body at the Incarnation. There are no bad things, only bad wills, [that is, acts of the will].

Chapter 16: SPAIN BECOMES A GREAT POWER   (Pages 203-213)

Completion

1. Asturias
2. Reconquista
3. Rodrigo Diaz
4. Alfonso VI
5. Moorish army; roads
6. Cordoba; Seville
7. Portuguese
8. army
9. Europe; Christ
10. Conversos; Moriscos
11. Inquisition
12. state; Church
13. Golden Age
14. East Indies; New World

Multiple Choice

1.	d	6.	a
2.	e	7.	c
3.	c	8.	a
4.	b	9.	c
5.	b	10.	c

True/False

1.	T	8.	F
2.	F	9.	T
3.	F	10.	T
4.	T	11.	T
5.	T	12.	F
6.	F	13.	T
7.	T		

Matching

1.	E	8.	C
2.	A	9.	K
3.	M	10.	D
4.	H	11.	I
5.	L	12.	G
6.	B	13.	F
7.	J		

Mini-Essay Question.

Criticism #1—The Inquisition used torture.

> Yes, it did, as did all governments of the time. This does not justify it, but the Inquisition should not be singled out for blame.

Criticism #2—The Inquisition's judgments led to the execution of the guilty.

> Yes, the guilty were traitors to both the state and the Church, and treason was punished with death. However, the guilty were given a chance to repent, and only if they refused to repent or relapsed into their crimes were they executed. Only 2,000 of the 100,000 tried were executed [see Publisher's Note below].

Criticism #3—The method of execution, burning at the stake, was an unusually barbaric form of execution. This was no more barbaric than the practices in France and England at the time, and Spain should not be singled out for condemnation. (*See p. 210-211.*)

[Publisher's Note: Since the publication of *Christ the King—Lord of History*, a mass of original records of the Spanish Inquisition has come to light, exonerating the Inquisition of the common charges against it. This evidence was presented in the 1994 BBC television documentary, "The Myth of the Spanish Inquisition," which stated: "Studying the archives of the Inquisition demolished the previous image that all of us had." Also, the Jewish historian Henry Kamen (*The Spanish Inquisition: A Historical Revision*, Yale Univ. Press, 1997) states: "Fewer people died from heresy in Spain than in any other Western country." In all of the 16th century in Spain and America the Inquisition "executed maybe forty or fifty people." (Quoted in *Why Apologize for the Spanish Inquisition?*, by Fr. Alphonsus Maria Duran, M.J. and Fr. Paul Mary Vota, M.J. [Chicago: Miles Jesu], 2000)].

Chapter 17: REVOLT AND COUNTERATTACK   (Pages 215-228)

Completion

1. classical civilization
2. humanism
3. Pope; wrongly
4. merit; grace
5. indulgence
6. community
7. Turks; Italy
8. Hapsburg
9. 36
10. anarchy
11. Knights'
12. Protestation
13. Ferdinand; Philip
14. God

Multiple Choice

1.	e	6.	b
2.	c	7.	d
3.	a	8.	c
4.	b	9.	a
5.	d	10.	b

True/False

1.	F	8.	T
2.	T	9.	T
3.	F	10.	T
4.	T	11.	F
5.	T	12.	F
6.	T	13.	T
7.	F		

Matching

1.	K	8.	L
2.	E	9.	C
3.	I	10.	M
4.	A	11.	B
5.	G	12.	H
6.	D	13.	J
7.	F		

Mini-Essay Question. They did not reform or improve anything in the Church. Instead they revolted or set themselves up against all existing authority, both spiritual and temporal.

Chapter 18: ENGLAND AGAINST THE FAITH   (Pages 230-242)

Completion

1. York; Lancaster
2. Bosworth; Tudor
3. annulment
4. Thomas Cromwell
5. Common
6. communion service
7. Mary Tudor
8. Martyrs
9. patriotism
10. treason; traitors
11. Protestant; Douai
12. priest; Eliot
13. Guise
14. Casket Letters

Multiple Choice

1.	b	6.	d
2.	c	7.	a
3.	a	8.	d
4.	b	9.	e
5.	c	10.	b

True/False

1.	T	8.	T
2.	F	9.	F
3.	T	10.	F
4.	T	11.	F
5.	F	12.	T
6.	F	13.	F
7.	T		

Matching

1.	E	8.	H
2.	J	9.	B
3.	K	10.	L
4.	G	11.	F
5.	M	12.	I
6.	C	13.	A
7.	D		

Mini-Essay Question. The "Bloody Mary" legend originated with Foxe's *Book of Martyrs*. Foxe was rabidly anti-Catholic, telling half-truths in order to present the case against Mary Tudor in the worst possible light. His book supposedly tells of 273 people "martyred" by Mary Tudor for their Protestant beliefs. He included the names of 169 persons listed by name only who were probably criminals who would have been executed under any monarch. That leaves 104 persons who were executed for a religion-related reason. However, Protestant leaders who were plotting against Mary were committing not only a religious offense, but were guilty of treason, a capital offense in any country. Foxe failed to mention that Henry VIII martyred 649, while Elizabeth martyred 189 in England and was responsible for the deaths of many more in Ireland. The name "Bloody Mary" is an example of anti-Catholic propaganda.

Chapter 19: THE CATHOLIC DEFENSE   (Pages 244-261)

Completion

1. St. Irenaeus; St. Martin
2. Calvinist Fury
3. Philip II
4. Duke of Alba
5. Act of Association
6. War of the Three Henries
7. France
8. O'Neill; O'Donnell
9. Irish
10. The Philippines
11. St. Bartholomew's Day Massacre
12. Siege of Malta
13. Protestants; Turks
14. Medina Sidonia

Multiple Choice

1.	c	6.	b
2.	c	7.	d
3.	e	8.	a
4.	a	9.	c
5.	d	10.	b

True/False

1.	T	8.	T
2.	F	9.	F
3.	F	10.	F
4.	T	11.	T
5.	T	12.	F
6.	T	13.	T
7.	F		

Matching

1.	H	8.	J
2.	C	9.	E
3.	F	10.	I
4.	A	11.	M
5.	G	12.	K
6.	B	13.	L
7.	D		

Mini-Essay Question. Catherine d'Medici turned to witchcraft and devil worship in order to bear children. She then bore several children. Although the children were responsible for their own souls, all of them either died early, were deformed, were ill in body or mind, or were very immoral.

Chapter 20: THE CATHOLIC OFFENSE   (Pages 264-274)

Completion

1. Catholic Reformation
2. Spiritual Exercises
3. Jesus; Jesuits
4. army; pope
5. defined
6. Pius V
7. Charles Borromeo
8. Carmelite
9. St. Francis Xavier
10. China
11. St. Francis Xavier
12. Japan
13. Guadalupe
14. Hernando Cortez

Multiple Choice

1.	b	6.	d
2.	c	7.	b
3.	d	8.	a
4.	d	9.	d
5.	c	10.	b

True/False

1.	F	8.	F
2.	T	9.	T
3.	F	10.	T
4.	F	11.	T
5.	T	12.	T
6.	F	13.	F
7.	T		

Matching

1.	H	8.	J
2.	G	9.	F
3.	E	10.	D
4.	I	11.	M
5.	A	12.	K
6.	B	13.	L
7.	C		

Mini-Essay Question. The Jesuits took a special vow of obedience to the Pope, promising to do whatever he asked of them. Martin Luther began a revolt under the auspices of a reformation. He was disobedient in many ways to the Pope and the Church. This revolt caused a division in the Church and began Protestantism.

Chapter 21: THE AGE OF FRANCE   (Pages 276-291)

Completion

1. seventeenth
2. Deism
3. Magisterium
4. France
5. Richelieu
6. Huguenots; Marie d'Medici
7. bureaucracy
8. Hapsburgs
9. Dutch; taxation
10. Mazarin
11. Canada
12. Christina
13. Czestochowa
14. Carlowitz

Multiple Choice

1.	b	6.	b
2.	a	7.	b
3.	d	8.	d
4.	c	9.	a
5.	a	10.	b

True/False

1.	T	8.	T
2.	F	9.	F
3.	T	10.	T
4.	F	11.	F
5.	F	12.	T
6.	F	13.	T
7.	F		

Matching

1.	H	8.	D
2.	J	9.	E
3.	G	10.	K
4.	A	11.	I
5.	M	12.	F
6.	L	13.	B
7.	C		

Mini-Essay Question. The Treaty of Westphalia marked the acceptance of a permanently split Christendom. Hence, nationalism became supreme, and the goal of each government was to gain as much power for itself as it could.

Chapter 22: THE RISE AND FALL OF THE STUARTS (Pages 294-308)

Completion

1. Gunpowder Plot
2. Pilgrims; Puritans
3. High
4. Preston
5. Interregnum
6. Test Act
7. Anne Hyde
8. Mary; Anne
9. Penal
10. Mass rocks; hedge schools
11. Jacobites
12. Charles; Henry
13. Cumberland
14. Protestantism; Parliament

Multiple Choice

1. d
2. d
3. c
4. c
5. a
6. a
7. b
8. e
9. a
10. c

True/False

1. F
2. T
3. T
4. T
5. F
6. F
7. T
8. T
9. T
10. F
11. F
12. F
13. T

Matching

1. M
2. J
3. B
4. D
5. K
6. A
7. L
8. I
9. E
10. C
11. G
12. H
13. F

Mini-Essay Question. 1) Parliament became dominant in England.
2) Protestantism was victorious over Catholicism in England.

Chapter 23: LIBERALS AND DESPOTS (Pages 310-321)

Completion

1. Freemasons
2. Rousseau
3. authority
4. Liberalism
5. united
6. Jesuits (or Society of Jesus)
7. enclosure
8. Relief
9. French and Indian
10. Poland
11. Pragmatic Sanction
12. army; courts
13. Krasinki; Pulaski
14. Russia

Multiple Choice

1. c
2. d
3. a
4. a
5. b
6. d
7. b
8. e
9. c
10. e

True/False

1. F
2. T
3. F
4. T
5. F
6. F
7. F
8. F
9. T
10. T
11. F
12. T
13. F

Matching

1. D
2. A
3. M
4. J
5. H
6. C
7. F
8. E
9. B
10. G
11. K
12. L
13. I

Mini-Essay Question. The eighteenth century is known as the Age of Reason or the Enlightenment on the theory that men had finally outgrown everything that hindered them from knowing truth and leading perfect lives (specifically, religious faith). They thought they would cure society of all that ailed it.

Chapter 24: THE FRENCH REVOLUTION (Pages 323-343)

Completion

1. Communism
2. noblemen; Liberals
3. Grievances
4. National Assembly
5. Bastille
6. God; majority
7. Jacobins
8. Varennes
9. non-juring
10. Austria
11. Vendee
12. Sunday; reason
13. Cisalpine
14. crosses; Sanfedisti

Multiple Choice

1. f
2. a
3. b
4. d
5. e
6. a
7. b
8. c
9. d
10. b

True/False

1. F
2. T
3. T
4. T
5. F
6. T
7. T
8. T
9. F
10. F
11. F
12. F
13. T

Matching

1. K
2. D
3. H
4. G
5. I
6. A
7. M
8. B
9. F
10. C
11. L
12. E
13. J

Mini-Essay Question. The liberals hated all authority. The Jacobins taught that everyone should have complete freedom to do whatever he wanted. These two positions were in harmony.

Chapter 25: THE AGE OF NAPOLEON (Pages 346-368)

Completion

1. Talleyrand; Fouche
2. Louisiana
3. Amiens
4. Trafalgar
5. Jena Auerstadt
6. Pius VII
7. Pillar Virgin
8. guerrilla
9. Tyrol
10. Russia
11. Vienna
12. Hundred Days
13. Congress; Carlsbad
14. Carlists

Multiple Choice

1.	d	6.	d
2.	c	7.	a
3.	b	8.	c
4.	c	9.	a
5.	b	10.	e

True/False

1.	T	8.	F
2.	T	9.	F
3.	F	10.	T
4.	F	11.	F
5.	T	12.	T
6.	T	13.	T
7.	F		

Matching

1.	E	8.	K
2.	D	9.	A
3.	J	10.	L
4.	M	11.	C
5.	B	12.	F
6.	G	13.	I
7.	H		

Mini-Essay Question. Metternich's ideas were consistent with the ideology of the Middle Ages, where right and wrong were determined by natural reason and Divine Law, not by majority rule. Metternich believed in maintaining order and respecting King and Church. Metternich knew that freedom came through order and authority. He said, "Without order as a foundation, the cry for freedom is nothing more than the attempt for some group or another to achieve its own ends. When actually carried out in practice, that freedom will inevitably express itself in tyranny." He believed in trying to settle controversies peaceably, maintaining a balance of power between nations so as not to go to war and watching that what was printed and taught was sound and did not promote revolutionary ideas. He worked very hard to build a society based on a respect for lawful authority (family, Church and King) and therefore subject to God's authority. He wanted all men to have freedom, which comes about when authority is able to maintain order.

Chapter 26: THE NINETEENTH CENTURY (Pages 370-390)

Completion

1. distributism
2. dialectic
3. Manifesto
4. robot
5. capitalism
6. Austria
7. Koniggratz
8. dual monarchy
9. kulturkampf
10. Republic
11. Prisoner
12. Imperialism
13. coffin
14. Rebellion

Multiple Choice

1.	a	6.	a
2.	c	7.	a
3.	c	8.	d
4.	c	9.	a
5.	b	10.	c

True/False

1.	F	8.	T
2.	F	9.	T
3.	T	10.	T
4.	F	11.	F
5.	T	12.	T
6.	F	13.	T
7.	F		

Matching

1.	M	8.	B
2.	A	9.	G
3.	K	10.	D
4.	I	11.	L
5.	E	12.	H
6.	J	13.	C
7.	F		

Mini-Essay Question. Most men used to own their own land or property so that they could be economically independent. After the Industrial Revolution, more people depended on a job in a business or factory. The wages paid the head of the family were not always enough to support it, so women and children would have to go to work too. Since the whole family was dependent on factory income, the factory owner could often take advantage of them, paying low wages and requiring long hours in poor conditions, because the family would starve if they quit.

Chapter 27: WORLD WAR I AND THE RUSSIAN REVOLUTION (Pages 393-413)

Completion

1. Dreyfus
2. Krupp
3. anarchist
4. Bloody; Nicholas
5. Schlieffen
6. Poland; Lithuania
7. Russia
8. Somme
9. Yusupov
10. Kerensky; seven
11. Bolsheviks; Lenin
12. Russia; Church
13. October; Whites
14. three

Multiple Choice

1. b   6. c
2. d   7. e
3. a   8. a
4. b   9. d
5. a   10. e

True/False

1. F   8. T
2. F   9. T
3. T   10. F
4. F   11. T
5. T   12. F
6. F   13. T
7. T

Matching

1. B   8. D
2. I   9. G
3. E   10. F
4. K   11. J
5. A   12. L
6. M   13. C
7. H

Mini-Essay Question.   The young men of Europe had been slaughtered by the millions. Europe was exhausted and disillusioned. Three ruling families—Hapsburg, Romanov, Hohenzollern—had been overthrown. Revolution had spread throughout Europe. The U.S. became a world power. A Communist dictatorship had been established in Russia.

Chapter 28: THE WORLD BETWEEN WARS   (Pages 416-427)

Completion

1. elected; Fourteen Points
2. Poland
3. Germans; Austrian Empire
4. Charles of Austria
5. League of Nations
6. Enabling
7. Catholic Church
8. Jesuits
9. Republicans; Nationalists
10. Cruzada
11. gold
12. Alcazar
13. trade; aid
14. Communists

Multiple Choice

1. d   6. e
2. b   7. c
3. d   8. c
4. c   9. c
5. a   10. c

True/False

1. F   8. F
2. T   9. F
3. T   10. F
4. T   11. F
5. T   12. T
6. T   13. T
7. T

Matching

1. F   8. E
2. I   9. D
3. C   10. H
4. K   11. J
5. A   12. B
6. L   13. G
7. M

Mini-Essay Question.

Criticism #1: Franco accepted aid from Nazi Germany.

Defense: Franco's army needed arms and weapons to fight against the revolutionaries (Communists), and the Germans (and Italians) were the only ones who would help him. Franco did not assist the Nazis in return, when World War II broke out. He did not help Hitler to obtain the strategic position of the Rock of Gibraltar, and Hitler's comment after the two met shows how uncooperative Franco was with him: "I would rather have all my teeth pulled than talk to that man again."

Criticism #2: Franco would not enter World War II on the Allied side.

Defense: Spain had been at war for three years already. The gold reserve had been severely depleted already by the revolutionaries. Franco could not put his people or his economy through more war. Spain needed peace and stability and that is what Franco brought her.

Chapter 29: WORLD WAR II (Pages 429-444)

Completion

1. Sudetenland
2. appeasement
3. Poland
4. Katyn
5. Dunkirk
6. Blitz
7. December 7, 1941
8. Ironbottom
9. Von Paulus
10. North Africa
11. saturation
12. Eastern Europe
13. Leyte
14. Maximilian Kolbe; starvation

Multiple Choice

1. e   6. b
2. c   7. c
3. d   8. a
4. a   9. a
5. d   10. d

True/False

1. T   8. F
2. F   9. T
3. F   10. T
4. T   11. F
5. T   12. F
6. T   13. T
7. F

Matching

1. I   8. F
2. E   9. C
3. M   10. B
4. J   11. H
5. A   12. D
6. G   13. L
7. K

Mini-Essay Question. (Note: The student may give any three of the following as answers to this Question.)

Along with prayer, Pope Pius XII took the following actions:

1. Using his diplomatic skills, he tried to forestall the war.
2. He issued many statements against Nazi policies and the persecution of Jews.
3. He permitted Vatican media to write and speak about Nazi atrocities in Poland.
4. On a death march of 20,000 Jews from Budapest to Theresienstadt, his Papal Nuncio (and Cardinal Seredi) organized relief vehicles to accompany the marchers with food and medicine and they rescued about 2,000 Jews with papal safe conduct passes.
5. His Papal Nuncio personally hid 200 Jews in his palace.
6. Pius XII instructed churches, monasteries, and convents in Rome to take in Jews.
7. He provided refuge for Jews in the Vatican itself.
8. He sent letters by hand to Italian bishops calling upon them to hide and rescue Jews.
9. He set up the Delasem organization to assist foreign Jews—4,000 Jews were assisted.

Note: Remember that the Catholic Church itself was a primary target of Hitler. Many, many Polish (and other) Catholics died in concentration camps along with their Jewish brothers and sisters. These numbers are not widely known, if they were even recorded, but the Church certainly opposed all extermination deaths.

Chapter 30: THE MODERN WORLD (Pages 447-462)

Completion

1. Winston Churchill; Josef Stalin
2. containment
3. Nationalists
4. Korean
5. Warsaw
6. Eisenhower
7. Cuba
8. Brazil; Chile
9. Ngo Dinh Diem
10. Portugal
11. Reagan
12. Boris Yeltsin
13. Africa
14. Modernism; Communism

Multiple Choice

1. a   6. e
2. b   7. d
3. e   8. a
4. d   9. d
5. d   10. d

True/False

1. F   8. F
2. T   9. T
3. T   10. F
4. T   11. T
5. T   12. T
6. T   13. T
7. F

Matching

1. L   8. A
2. M   9. B
3. J   10. D
4. K   11. F
5. C   12. H
6. E   13. G
7. I

Mini-Essay Question. Roosevelt and Churchill agreed to give Russia a dominant influence over Poland in return for Stalin's help in winning the war against Japan (and for his support of the United Nations). However, Great Britain had actually gone to war against Germany to preserve Poland's independence. So it was unfair that Poland's independence was given away in return for Stalin's help in winning the war against Japan, especially when the Soviet Union was not even needed to defeat Japan.